my father's daughter

my father's daughter

DELICIOUS, EASY RECIPES CELEBRATING

FAMILY & TOGETHERNESS

gwyneth paltrow

Foreword by Mario Batali
Photographs by Ellen Silverman

GRAND CENTRAL
Life & Style
NEW YORK • BOSTON

Grand Central Life & Style
Hachette Book Group
237 Park Avenue
New York, NY 10017

www.HachetteBookGroup.com

Grand Central Life & Style is an imprint
of Grand Central Publishing.
The Grand Central Life & Style name
and logo are trademarks of Hachette
Book Group, Inc.

Printed in the United States of America

First Edition: April 2011
10 9 8 7 6 5 4 3 2 1

Library of Congress Cataloging-in-
Publication Data
Paltrow, Gwyneth, 1972–
My father's daughter : delicious,
easy recipes celebrating family and
togetherness / Gwyneth Paltrow.—1st ed.
    p. cm.
  Includes index.
  ISBN 978-0-446-55731-3
  1. Cooking, American. 2. Cookbooks.
3. Paltrow, Gwyneth, 1972—Family. I. Title.
  TX715.P1846 2011
  641.5973—dc22
          2010036507

DESIGN BY LAURA PALESE
ILLUSTRATIONS BY DANIELLE DESCHENES

this book is dedicated to

my brother, Jake, my first guinea pig, who makes meals great just by being there, and for looking so much like Bruce while he is eating them. Also to our closest friends, our family really, who are always the reason to have a dinner party, the Wigmore-Reynolds, the Van Nices, the Carters, the Turly-Burnses and their extended clan, the Maudes, the Harveys, the Downeys, the McCartney-Willises, the Spielbergs, the Nadal-Saxe-Coburgs, the Conrad-Manions, the Hill-McGraws…

for Apple and Moses, hearts of my artichoke, my raisins d'être

author's note

I literally could not have written this book without the tireless, artful assistance of Julia Turshen, who stood over my shoulder at the stove and chopping block for the better part of a year, bringing a method to my freestyling madness. She quantified, tested, and retested every recipe, oversaw the production of the photos, helped brainstorm in a crisis, and, above all, was my intellectual and emotional support through the whole process.

contents

foreword

BY MARIO BATALI

In all great cultures on Terra Madre, food and family are deeply intertwined with tradition, pleasure, and responsibility. Although it is only in the last couple of decades that Americans have awakened to the complexity and magnificence of our own gastronomic quilt—a pastiche of an infinite variety of cultures and delicious (relatively) young and modern gastronomic traditions—it has not dampened our intense fervor or our appetite for both the food and the history of our own families and heritage, even if cobbled together over a single generation. Although the Paltrows and the Batalis are relatively recent friends—of only twelve years—our approach to our family traditions is similarly sacred, and our intents and appreciations equal in both intensity and pleasure.

My family's historic events, major celebrations, and even simple holidays have always been punctuated not only by food but by specific dishes. Christmas Eve at Grandma and Grandpa Batali's house was a series of traditional fish dishes, the same every year. Long before I knew or cared about the sacraments of the Catholic faith, I knew that the odd-smelling baccala and tomato sauce simmering on the back of the stove in Grandma's kitchen would be served with polenta and that crab would also be a part of our meal. That Grandma served the salad after the main course was always perceived as her forgetfulness, not her strategy and her family tradition from Abruzzo. When she dipped her biscotti into her wine after dinner, we thought she was nuts and laughed with her about the seemingly odd and wacky move.

Traveling with Gwyneth or sharing dinner with her at a restaurant or in our homes, I realized that her family's gastronomic traditions were as feverishly loved and observed as those in my family. Her passion for the delicious and her delightful and even obsessive curiosity went beyond simply eating good food. She also discovered and savored its historical perspective and relevance. These are two of the reasons we decided to pursue our shared love of Spain in the PBS series *Spain…On the Road Again*.

To eat with someone who loves food can double the fun. To eat with Gwyneth is even more than that. Let's put aside the fact that GP can effortlessly down a whole pan of perfect paella in Valencia or eat an entire plate of marinated anchovies in Barcelona. She simply loves not only the "deliciousness" of each bite, but the fact that the ritual of the table is in itself a celebration. And when food, and its preparation, becomes so much more than mere nourishment, when it becomes entertainment and folly and libidinal pleasure all rolled into one thing? At that point every meal, every snack, every shared moment of sustenance can be a celebration. And it should be—not in a super serious way where overthinking can drain the fun from these moments, but in a carefree, sunrise-happy way.

Watching Gwyneth blossom as a mom cook has been fascinating. Her "flexitarianism" has never been an issue in the family, and I do not think that her children think for a moment they are eating a "special" way other than the fact that they know the shared meal itself is a special moment. They certainly do not eat "fast" food or processed evil and will probably enjoy better health in the long run because of that. Either that or become junk food junkies in their rebellious teens as a result!

The fundamental generosity of cooking for others is a very special role for the mom who loves to cook and eat. The concept of nurturing is a learned one, and clearly GP's whole clan (actually, BOTH her natural family and her Spanish adopted family too!) shared this belief. If this book has been a delicious exercise of introspection and documentation for Gwyneth, then the creation of the website/blog GOOP.com has crystallized her point of view in the public domain. The intersection of the two is what we cooking enthusiasts can harvest as we think about and more importantly…ENJOY!

The most important thing to take from *My Father's Daughter* is the true pleasure we can derive from the thinking about, then the making of, and finally the enjoyment of eating good food together with people we care about.

The best way to truly understand this book? Take the Perfect Roasted Chinese Duck recipe (page 179) and follow the careful instructions to the T. Eat it with some people you love.

LIVE LARGE!

"To eat with someone who loves food can double the fun. To eat with Gwyneth is even more than that."

introduction

Why? you may ask. In the last ten years or so, cooking has become my main ancillary passion in life. I have always loved food, being around it, preparing it, and of course eating it. This adoration was instilled in me by my incredible father, a supreme gourmand with a deep love for great food and wine.

I always feel closest to my father, who was the love of my life until his death in 2002, when I am in the kitchen. I can still hear him over my shoulder, heckling me, telling me to be careful with my knife, moaning with pleasure over a bite of something in the way only a Jew from Long Island can, his shoulders doing most of the talking. I will never forget how concentrated he looked in the kitchen, it almost looked like a grimace or a frown if you didn't know him. He practiced incredible care and precision when he was preparing food. It was as if the deliciousness of the food would convey the love he felt in direct proportion.

He and I were always inseparable. When I was a baby, my mother was essentially the breadwinner in our house while my father was trying to rustle up a career in television. He walked me in his arms all night long as, by all accounts, I never slept. He took me everywhere with him, to each meeting and each diner, always ready to supply me with my fix of Red Cheek apple juice. We went to Jewish delicatessens and to now-extinct drive-ins where I was introduced to the finer points of the egg cream and the ice cream float. Health food was never really on the agenda; it was about fun and deliciousness and togetherness.

When I was a kid in Santa Monica, California, he often took us out to eat in what was then the start of the "California cuisine" era, taking great pride in my brother and me eating what would have been unheard of for him as a kid (oysters, artichokes, blue cheese, anything French). He looked forward to going out for a family meal with the genuine excitement of someone who never grew up eating in restaurants, and somehow that happiness, when we were all getting in the car, never seemed to wear off, no matter how many times we went to Michael's or 72 Market Street. For years, this excitement for food was limited to dining out—there wasn't a lot of agonizing over the home menu or tons of shopping and chopping. But that would change. Looking back, I think it all started with the pancakes.

My father was a master pancake maker. To the point that anyone who ever tried them would vouch that they were the best they had ever had. They still will to this day. They were thin, and light, and had that perfect subtle tang from fresh buttermilk. The pancake making started as a casual weekend breakfast thing and became a ritual. He became obsessed with perfecting them, eventually making the batter the night before as he was convinced it had some discreet effect on the outcome. Not only would we, his children and wife, delight in the taste of those mini stacks with warmed up maple syrup, but our extended family of friends would as well, the size of the group often swelling to twenty or so. I think he started to feel the impact of making people so content and relaxed and sated with those pancakes. He was, after all, the most loving and nurturing of all men.

When I was about eighteen we started cooking together. I'm not sure exactly how it started, what day it was, or how it was catalyzed. I just remember that we were both living back in Santa Monica (I was trying to get work as an actress and was hostessing in a fish restaurant) and we got tired of the giant supply of spaghetti and meatballs my mother had very kindly made and left in the freezer since she was working in New York. We decided to make a meal, and from there we got kind of obsessed. We would watch the cooking channel together as much as we watched NFL football, often with me resting in the crook of his arm. We would call each other with things we had learned, compare tips, recipes, and ideas like making salad dressing by putting all the ingredients into a little glass jar and shaking it up (utterly revolutionary to us at the time) or dicing an onion by cutting it in half vertically, making small slices vertically, then cutting horizontally, essentially eliminating the "chopping." "What kind of moron am I that I nevah thought of this!" he would say in his heavily accented New York–ese.

My father's meals got more layered and more complex in lots of ways, and, in other ways, he stuck to his basic greatest hits. The most striking aspect of his cooking was how much joy he derived from feeding people that he loved. I mean, genuine, bursting happiness. And he instilled in me the idea that a meal made for your family is an expression of love, a source of pleasure—not only in the visceral enjoyment of the food, but also in the magic that is created when you imbue food with energy and nurturing.

I understood him more fully when I had my own children. Over the years I had learned how to cook through trial and error, through cooking classes, through lessons with chef friends, but it had always been for fun. Now it seemed much more, well, *important.* Unlike my daddy, who back in the day thought Oreos and a glass of milk were snack worthy, I became a bit obsessed with providing my kids with healthy, unprocessed foods. This was informed by a period of eating a strictly macrobiotic diet, which, ironically enough, I had started when my father was diagnosed with throat cancer in the fall of 1998. I was devastated by his diagnosis and became convinced that he could heal himself with good foods and alternative medicine, even if he was resistant to the (perhaps naive) idea. I armed myself by reading anything available that linked processed foods, pesticides, growth hormones, preservatives, and the like to cancer and other diseases. I enlisted a macrobiotic counselor who had healed herself from cancer by eating a "healing diet" and also even brought on a chef to get us started. I was dealing with a man who upon hearing his cancer diagnosis went out for hot dogs and after an excruciating throat surgery wanted to go straight to Mr. Chow. I think that he equated his beloved morning coffee with two sugars to being "normal" and never embraced the idea of cutting anything out even if it would have made a difference in his health in the long run.

But all the information that I gathered did make a big personal impact. I learned about how the body can heal itself from almost anything. I learned about the physical and environmental effects of pesticides. I went strictly organic, local, and macro and eliminated dairy, sugar, meat, liquor, gluten, all (I think) in a bid to heal my father by proxy. Of course I couldn't cure him, but I found that my body felt really good. I loved eating this way and I stuck to it for years, although sometimes, damn, I just wanted a slice of coffee cake or a martini with olives.

When I was pregnant a few years later, I could not eat a bowl of brown rice for love or money. I wanted grilled cheese sandwiches and Baskin-Robbins Jamoca Almond Fudge ice cream, and, well, you can guess what won out. But when my daughter started eating solid food, the pendulum swung and again I focused on organic and whole foods. I did not want her to ingest pesticides, herbicides, growth hormones, antibiotics, or preservatives and I still don't. In fact, sometimes I wonder if my father would still be alive today if he hadn't grown up eating so much of that stuff.

Through this process my father and daughter had unwittingly taught me the importance of balance. Could I use some butter and cheese and eggs in my cooking without going down some kind of hippie shame spiral? Yes. Of course I could. I would go back to eating chicken, but only once in a while and it would be free range and organic. I would support my local farmers always, but if I needed some tomatoes in winter to slowly roast for soup, I would go to the supermarket.

This idea of balance became just an easing up on myself, which is something I find challenging to this day. On a broader scale, I try to remember this balance when I think about being a working mother. How do I cook for my family, do the school run, work on my projects, exercise, and not lose out on a great film project? I can't. And that's okay. Because my instincts have been shaped by a man who knew that family was everything. And my family will always be where I strive most for success. Making a home, cooking with love, and bringing everyone together are my tangible ways of achieving that kind of success.

My father, even through his deteriorating health in the aftermath of his cancer surgery, when his beloved red wine burned his throat and he struggled to chew and swallow, showed me through his own enjoyment that gathering around a table is the high point of the day. Through shared meals and meaningful togetherness, he made happiness feel achievable. He helped me realize it's all about the here and now, that happiness happens on a freezing winter night or in the garden when the weather's warm, often with a good bottle of wine, and always with the people you love. You just need some good ingredients and a few simple recipes, maybe a couple of jokes, or a "topic to dissect" at the table, the way they do at Nora Ephron's house.

And there it is. It's what I believe in. In these pages you will find recipes for simple, (mostly) healthy, delicious food. This is the food I cook for my family and friends, over and over again, the food that never fails me. This book is meant to channel the ethos of my father by sharing the greatest gifts that he imparted to me. Invest in what's real. Clean as you go. Drink while you cook. Make it fun. It doesn't have to be complicated. It will be what it will be.

why i don't eat red meat

I was raised a red meat lover; I lived for brisket, ribs, meatballs, and especially Bolognese sauce. When I was twenty-one, a friend gave me a book called *Diet for a New America* by John Robbins, which exposed the brutal practices of American factory farms. Reading this book gave me a whole new perspective on what I was eating. That, coupled with a lecture I got from Leonardo DiCaprio (when he was nineteen and I was twenty-one) about how such animals are kept and processed, made me lose my desire for factory farm pork and beef right there. I do, however, eat poultry. I always try to buy birds that are from farms where they are raised cage-free and organic. Chickens are victims of some of the worst factory-farming practices, so if it's not naturally raised, think twice.

MY CHILDREN'S MOTHER

Including my children in all aspects culinary is very important to me and always has been. When my daughter, Apple, was born in 2004, I always had her strapped to my chest in one of those BabyBjörn things and later on my hip in the kitchen while I stirred and chopped, one handed at that! Soon she was sitting up and I had fantasies of an extra-high high chair on wheels so she could be out of harm's way but privy to the action as I steamed and pureed her baby food. She was always trying to get a glimpse inside the pot, fascinated by the sounds of simmering and frying, or reaching to hold the big wooden spoon, mystified by its meaning (drumstick? teething device?).

Children are inherently curious about the process of cooking—it's mysterious and vaguely threatening, and seemingly for adults only. Fire and knives, no wonder my son is obsessed with it all. He, like my daughter, loves nothing more than helping me cook a meal. The trick is to let them participate as long as they are interested; eventually they wander off and busy themselves with something else, but lately they've been staying with it.

I believe it is the fact that I am carefully letting them do things that seem beyond their level that keeps them so interested. Whenever I am holding my son so that he can add salt to a sauce or stir something (with a long handle from a safe distance), I regularly think of some parenting advice my father gave on one occasion. His theory was that children positively respond to being trusted with something that they don't expect you to trust them with. And when they are trusted and complete something successfully, not only is their self-esteem buoyed but so is the connection between parent and child. Thus is my willingness to allow them to partake in some of the more adult tasks, with very careful supervision.

The three of us regularly engage in cooking together and doing this is one of my all-time favorite activities—all immersed in a project together, having fun, and making dinner! It is a multitasker's dream, genuine quality time spent while checking something off the list.

1. Turn the pepper grinder.
2. Add pinches of salt and other spices.
3. Stir batters and doughs in mixing bowls.
4. Spread butter on toast.
5. Grease cake pans.
6. Line muffin tins.
7. Crack eggs.
8. Whisk dressings.
9. Press the start button on appliances (with supervision, of course).
10. Add items to a blender, mixing bowl, etc.
11. Level off flour, sugar, etc.
12. Crush garlic in a press. (Watch their fingers!)

It is my belief that children should know about food, should learn how to handle and prepare it. I think of it as a life skill no less important than any other…maybe more so as it will enable them to take control of their health as they get older. They have become well versed in their own likes and they often have opinions about how things are done.

Here are some of the ways that I include them in the process, ways you might be able to incorporate into your routine.

1. Go to the farmers' market or supermarket together. Give your children their own baskets and ask them to pick out vegetables or grains or fish that look interesting to them, anything that is fresh or dried, not processed. Look up recipes using the ingredients they have selected and have them choose something appealing to them. Easy books that focus on ingredient-driven, simple preparations are great (like *River Cafe Cookbook Easy*, by Rose Gray and Ruth Rogers, and Alice Waters's *The Art of Simple Food*, or look at epicurious.com or other foodie websites). If they are old enough, have them assist in the washing and preparing of the food. My kids beam with pride when they have had an impact on a family meal.

2. Make a kitchen garden. Go to your local nursery for young plants or peruse the Internet for seeds you can order. Kids love the process of watching things grow, especially when the choice of herb or vegetable was their idea. Plant veggies or herbs in a patch if you have a garden or even in pots by a sunny window or on a fire escape. Watering plants and checking their growth with a ruler is always fun. Get little veggie- and herb-picking baskets for them and have them do the cutting and picking themselves. (You will be surprised how well baby scissors work on a bunch of chives.)

3. Talk about the seasonality of the food, why and how things grow in different temperatures. Get a list of what grows when, starting with the season you are currently in. Narrow down the list to three or four of the fruits and vegetables in season and talk about appealing ways to cook them. Go to local farms or join a co-op where you can pick what is growing. Do a bit of history on a food that is not native to your area and ask your kids to think about how it gets to your kitchen from where it has come from.

4. Make treats from scratch. Kids love carbs carbs carbs and so they should, they are delicious. In my kitchen we love to deep-fry French fries, so I make sure we do it often enough to satisfy cravings, but not every day or even every week. I always use organic vegetable oil and potatoes to try to convince myself that the French fries are healthy. Maybe not, but at least I know where the main ingredients are coming from. I try to alternate less healthy cravings with healthy options as well: baked sweet potato fries still taste great with ketchup and are a much healthier alternative to deep-fried potatoes. Whole wheat pasta and brown rice are easily dressed up with a flavorful sauce. For sweet treats, the homemade version will always trump a store-bought variety, which will always contain preservatives and other unsavory ingredients. And always let the kids lick the bowl in reward for their concentration and hard work!

5. Expose your kids to the flavors of other countries and cultures. One fun way to do this is to ask your kids about what they think children are eating in a far-off land. Do some research about popular dishes and see what sounds interesting to them. Then make a menu plan and cook a meal with a theme from, for example, Mexico, Japan, or Thailand—the options are endless—and you can try a different country every week. You can even listen to music from the country for extra inspiration.

6. Have your kids measure out ingredients. It's a great way to hone developing math skills. If something calls for a cup of flour, I often hand my daughter a one-third-cup measuring cup and ask her how many of these she needs to put in the bowl to add up to one cup. You can make this as challenging or simple as suits your family.

how to
use this book

To help you decide which recipes to make depending on your schedule and
who you are cooking for, I've added icons to each recipe. Here is the key:

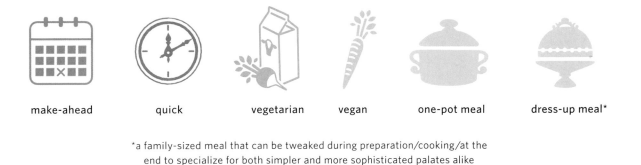

| make-ahead | quick | vegetarian | vegan | one-pot meal | dress-up meal* |

*a family-sized meal that can be tweaked during preparation/cooking/at the
end to specialize for both simpler and more sophisticated palates alike

There are also notes on some recipes: "Make It Vegan" or "Make It Kid Friendly"
that offer you flexibility depending on your and your children's preferences.

trust yourself I am not a professional cook. I am an amateur and a lover of all things
culinary. I learned to cook with trial and mostly error. Over the years I have learned three essential
things: control your heat—watch the fire carefully, flavors are usually diminished by things cooking too
quickly (though there are exceptions)—trust yourself, and taste as you go. When you approach a meal
with fear that it's going to be terrible, it probably will be. Approach it like it is going to be delicious. And
don't forget the importance of the seasoning—that last pinch of salt or squeeze of lemon—especially
when you're preparing simple, ingredient-driven food—can be the most important step.

the well-stocked
pantry

Oddly, some of the most exhilarating creative moments I experience take place when I stand in the kitchen faced with the task of making dinner when I wasn't expecting to. For the cook who comes home from work and hasn't had time to go shopping, the importance of the well-stocked pantry is paramount. The pantry for me isn't just dried and canned goods. I make sure to have fresh things with a good shelf life—garlic, onions, shallots, root vegetables, as well as homemade prepared items I always keep in my fridge—Slow-Roasted Tomatoes (page 32), Basic Tomato Sauce (page 30), along with celery, leeks, and carrots, and herbs wrapped in damp towels. With a well-stocked pantry, great meals can be completely spontaneous.

OPPOSITE, FROM LEFT TO RIGHT: dark agave nectar, light agave nectar, honeycomb, maple syrup, manuka honey, brown rice syrup

ESSENTIAL FOOD ITEMS
TO KEEP IN YOUR KITCHEN

Oils

Olive (I especially like extra virgin olive oil from Spain and Italy.)

Canola (good for baking and dressings)

Safflower and peanut (good for frying)

Grapeseed (great for dressings)

Toasted sesame and hot pepper sesame (good for flavoring)

Vinegars

Mostly I use red and white wine vinegar, but a variety, including balsamic, rice wine, sherry, and champagne, is lovely to have on hand.

Condiments and Sauces

Vegenaise (My most often-used and beloved ingredient. It can be found at most grocery stores and all health food stores—unfortunately not yet in London. Regular mayo is fine and works, but Vegenaise is a healthier alternative.)

Dijon mustard

Coarse, seeded mustard

Tomato paste

Cholula hot sauce

Sriracha (commercial or homemade, see page 35)

Miso (white, barley, and red)

Unsweetened peanut butter

Good jams and preserves (including ginger, raspberry, blueberry, and apricot)

Real Vermont maple syrup

Mirin

Fish sauce

Soy sauce

Bragg Liquid Aminos

Canned Goods

Canned tuna (packed in olive oil)

Anchovies!

Beans (including kidney, black, cannellini, and butter beans)

Canned whole peeled tomatoes with their juice

Rices, Pastas, Legumes

Dried lentils

Pastas (including spaghetti, penne, pappardelle, rigatoni, macaroni, and whole wheat pasta)

Soba noodles

Short-grain brown rice

Bomba rice (for paella)

Go-To Produce

Onions (yellow and red)

Garlic

Fresh ginger

Lemons

Celery

Carrots

Herbs (including basil, parsley, cilantro, and chives)

In the Fridge

Organic butter

Organic large eggs

Bacon (I use a lot of turkey and duck bacon.)

Cheese (including Parmigiano-Reggiano and other hard cheeses that will last the longest if wrapped properly in an airtight container or plastic wrap, also Gorgonzola, mozzarella—which lasts only for two to three days—and sharp Cheddar)

In the Freezer

Stocks
> Vegetable Stock (page 36)
> Fish Stock (page 40)
> Chicken Stock (page 39)

Ice cream

Frozen vegetables (including peas, corn, and edamame)

For Baking

Arrowroot starch or cornstarch

Baking soda

Baking powder

Light agave nectar

Brown rice syrup

Flours (including white spelt, whole spelt, buckwheat, and unbleached all-purpose)

Sugars (including unrefined dark brown, confectioners', and granulated cane)

Vanilla beans and/or extract

The Spice Shelf

Maldon salt

Coarse or kosher salt

Garam masala

Celery seeds

Cinnamon (whole and ground)

Cumin (whole and ground)

Chili powder

Red chile flakes

Fennel seeds

Coriander seeds

Nutmeg

Black peppercorns

Pimenton (Spanish smoked paprika)

Dried whole chiles

Saffron

Cloves (whole and ground)

Ground ginger

Wasabi powder

Some Other Ingredients

Bonito flakes, kombu, wakame, and kimchi (found in Asian grocery stores or online—see page 266)

Salt-packed capers

King Arthur bread flour or 00 flour (both the higher-protein "bread" and "pasta" varieties for pizza and pasta doughs—found in Italian specialty markets or online)

Nuts (including almonds, walnuts, and pecans)

Seeds (including sunflower, pumpkin, and sesame)

Dried fruit (including raisins and cranberries)

RECIPES FOR STOCKS, SAUCES & SPECIAL INGREDIENTS

basic tomato sauce

THIS SAUCE IS A SIMPLE, perfect tomato sauce. Slow cooked to bring out the sweetness, it is the perfect base for many things in this book and delicious on its own with some penne or spaghetti. My daughter eats this maybe slightly too often…my son prefers pesto.

2 tablespoons extra virgin olive oil

6 cloves garlic, peeled and thinly sliced

4 fresh large basil leaves

2 28-ounce cans whole peeled tomatoes with their juice

Coarse salt

Freshly ground black pepper

Heat the olive oil in a large saucepan over low heat, add the garlic, and cook for 5 minutes. Add 2 of the basil leaves and stir for a minute. Add the tomatoes and their juice and the 2 remaining basil leaves. Turn the heat to high. Bring the sauce to a boil, turn the heat to low, season with salt and pepper, and let it bubble away on low heat for 45 minutes, stirring occasionally and crushing the tomatoes with your wooden spoon. Cool and refrigerate.

 YIELD: 4 cups · ACTIVE PREPARATION TIME: 15 minutes
TOTAL PREPARATION TIME: 1 hour

roasted bell peppers

ROASTED RED PEPPERS WERE AMONG the first antipasti my father learned to prepare (and with great pride). In his version, after roasting, sweating, and peeling the peppers, he would marinate them in olive oil and (painfully) thinly sliced garlic overnight. The next day he would bring them back to room temperature, lay some anchovies over the top, and finish with a scattering of coarsely chopped Italian parsley. He would serve them with a massive smile on his face, like he really had gotten this gourmet thing down. They are great to have on hand to serve up à la Bruce, in a roast veggie sandwich or panini, or atop a salad niçoise.

Roast whole bell peppers over an open gas flame on high heat, rotating with tongs, until completely blackened all over. Be patient—you want the flesh to soften and the skin to be totally, totally charred; it should take 15 or 20 minutes. After the peppers are cooked, put them in a large metal or glass bowl, cover it with plastic wrap, and let them sit until they're cool enough to handle (the covered bowl creates steam which makes it super easy to peel the peppers). Incidentally, a plastic bag works too.

When they're cool, slip off and discard the charred skins, running them under water as needed to remove all the skin. Cut the peppers open and discard the seeds. These keep for 1–2 weeks well rubbed with a little olive oil and stored in an airtight container in the refrigerator.

YIELD: flexible • **ACTIVE PREPARATION TIME:** ½ hour • **TOTAL PREPARATION TIME:** 1 hour

vanilla bean sugar

SWEET RECIPES ALWAYS BENEFIT from using real vanilla beans, their beautiful paste scraped out, adding those delightful black flecks to batter, French toast, anything your heart desires. Instead of throwing the empty pods in the bin or compost, I add them to a jar of organic sugar, which is then infused with the vanilla flavor, nice when baking.

slow-roasted tomatoes

A PANTRY ESSENTIAL. THIS METHOD turns even the most flavorless out-of-season winter tomatoes into gorgeous, sweet ones. I always have them in the fridge to brighten up sandwiches, salads, cheese plates, and the like.

Vine-ripened tomatoes

Olive oil

Salt

Preheat the oven to 275°F.

Cut the tomatoes in half horizontally, rub with a tiny bit of olive oil and a pinch of salt and bake seed side up in a 275°F oven for 3–5 hours, or until they look nearly sun dried (the edges will be caramelized and the moisture will be almost entirely evaporated). These keep, well refrigerated in an airtight container with a bit of olive oil, for at least a week, so make a whole bunch at once.

 YIELD: flexible • ACTIVE PREPARATION TIME: 5 minutes
TOTAL PREPARATION TIME: 3–5 hours

"I'm not gluten free but I like gluten-free food."

—APPLE

lee's homemade sriracha

LEE GROSS IS A (MOSTLY) MACROBIOTIC chef I have known and worked with at various times over the past decade. He was the chef who taught me about macrobiotics around the time that my father became ill and I got hell bent on the family eating better. Trained by Michio Kushi at the Kushi Institute in Becket, Massachusetts, and at Johnson & Wales in Rhode Island, Lee beautifully fuses the concepts of healthy and delicious. He has taught me a world of food knowledge that I apply all the time. One day when I was talking about my love for this spicy, smoky condiment, he informed me that it was full of chemicals. Luckily he came up with this version, which is just as delicious and preservative free! Don't worry—it still keeps for ages in the fridge.

1¼ cups peeled cloves garlic

1 pound red jalapeños, stemmed and sliced into thin rings (remove some seeds for a milder sauce)

2¼ cups rice wine vinegar

¼ cup plus 1 tablespoon light agave nectar

2 tablespoons coarse salt

1 tablespoon arrowroot powder

2 tablespoons fish sauce (or you can substitute soy sauce if you are vegetarian)

Put the garlic in a small saucepan and add cold water just to cover. Bring to a boil, immediately drain, cool the garlic under running water, and return it to the saucepan. Cover with cold water and repeat the blanching process. Thinly slice the blanched garlic and combine with the jalapeños and vinegar in a larger pot. Bring to a boil, cook for 3 minutes, and remove from the heat. Add the agave and salt and stir to combine. Let mixture sit undisturbed for 1 hour to steep and cool.

Whiz the mixture in a blender until smooth (it's okay if all the seeds don't blend in). Return the pureed sauce to the pot, bring to a boil, lower the heat, and simmer for 10–15 minutes, skimming any foam as necessary, until the sauce is slightly reduced and has some body.

In a small bowl, dissolve the arrowroot with 1 tablespoon of lukewarm water. Whisk into the simmering sauce and cook for 2 minutes more, or until the sauce is nicely thickened (it should be slightly thinner than ketchup). Remove the sauce from the heat, let cool slightly, and stir in the fish sauce.

YIELD: 5 cups • ACTIVE PREPARATION TIME: 30 minutes • TOTAL PREPARATION TIME: 2 hours

vegetable stock

GOOD STOCK IS ESSENTIAL to have in your freezer. As vegetable stock out of a box can be completely insipid, I started making and freezing this robust stock since it brings vegetarian soups and stuffings up a notch.

1 large yellow onion, peeled and roughly chopped

2 large carrots, peeled and roughly chopped

1 stalk celery, roughly chopped

1 large leek, roughly chopped

3 cloves garlic, peeled and whacked with the back of your knife

4 sprigs fresh parsley

4 sprigs fresh thyme

2 sprigs fresh tarragon

1 bay leaf

1 teaspoon coarse salt

1 teaspoon black peppercorns

3 quarts cold water

Combine everything in a pot. Bring to a boil, lower the heat, and simmer for 45 minutes. Let it cool and strain into a clean container.

Keeps 1–2 weeks in the fridge, 6 months in the freezer.

YIELD: 3 quarts · **ACTIVE PREPARATION TIME:** 10 minutes
TOTAL PREPARATION TIME: 1 hour plus cooling

chicken stock

THIS STRAIGHTFORWARD CHICKEN STOCK is foolproof and makes a great base. Make sure to use organic chicken!

1   organic whole chicken, washed and dried (See Salt Scrubs for Poultry, page 43.)

1   teaspoon black peppercorns

1   bay leaf

2   stalks celery, roughly chopped

1   large yellow onion, peeled and roughly chopped

2   carrots, peeled and roughly chopped

3   sprigs fresh parsley

3   sprigs fresh thyme

1   teaspoon coarse salt

Put all of the ingredients into a large soup pot, cover with cold water (should take about 3 quarts), and bring to a boil over high heat. Skim any foam that rises to the top, turn the heat down to low, and simmer for 1½ hours. Let the stock cool and then strain into containers to freeze. The chicken makes for great chicken salad or you can shred it into the strained broth, add a couple of carrots cut into coins and some diced celery, and enjoy some delicious soup.

Keeps 1–2 weeks in the fridge, 6 months in the freezer.

YIELD: about 10 cups · **ACTIVE PREPARATION TIME:** 10 minutes
TOTAL PREPARATION TIME: 2 hours plus cooling

fish stock

FISH STOCK IS ESSENTIAL for paella, fish soups, and risottos. Make a large quantity and freeze it. As with other stocks, it really comes in handy—especially if you are cooking last minute.

Shells from 4 lobsters or shells and heads of 6 shrimp (I keep them in a plastic bag in the freezer after a special dinner.)

1 halibut frame (or any other bones from not-too-oily fish; ask your fishmonger—he should be happy to give them to you)

2 stalks celery, roughly chopped

1 yellow onion, peeled and roughly chopped

1 large leek, thoroughly cleaned and roughly chopped

3 carrots, peeled and roughly chopped

2 bay leaves

3 sprigs fresh parsley

1 tablespoon peppercorns

1 tablespoon coarse salt or Maldon sea salt

Combine everything in a large pot and cover with cold water. Bring to a boil, skim any foam that rises to the surface, lower the heat, and simmer for 25–30 minutes. Let the stock cool and then strain it into containers for the freezer or use it immediately for a soup or a paella.
Keeps 1–2 weeks in the fridge, 6 months in the freezer.

YIELD: about 5 quarts · **ACTIVE PREPARATION TIME:** 10 minutes
TOTAL PREPARATION TIME: 40 minutes plus cooling

THE ESSENTIAL TOOLS

1 **Vitamix blender** (This will make your soups creamy with no added cream, make smoothies extra light, make bread crumbs and dressings and more, all at variable speeds. Worth the investment, it will last forever and change your life.)

2 **Microplane grater**

3 **Steamer** (Black & Decker makes a great model that sits on your counter. Or a simple bamboo steamer works well.)

4 **Global knives**

5 **Knife sharpener**

6 **Jamie Oliver Flavour Shaker**

7 **OrGreenic nonstick pans**

8 **Le Creuset Dutch oven**

9 **Stainless steel cookware** (All-Clad is my favorite.)

10 Butcher block counter

11 Pyrex glass bowls

12 Wooden spoons

13 Earthenware baking dishes

14 Good corkscrew

15 Wine Saver

16 KitchenAid mixer

17 KitchenAid pasta roller attachment

18 Cheap stainless steel bowls

19 Half sheet pans

PREPPING TECHNIQUES
FOR POULTRY & CLAMS

salt scrubs for poultry

Before I cook a chicken or a duck, I always wash it carefully. First I wet it with cold water and then I scrub it with a handful of coarse kosher or rock salt. Then I rinse it with more water and pat it completely dry, inside and out, with paper towels. My grandmother Dorothy (my father's mother) called it "koshering" a chicken, although I'm not sure it's possible to do that after the fact...

salt scrubs for clams

I once learned a great way to clean clams. First you fill a bowl with cold water and let the clams soak for about ten minutes. Then drain them, sprinkle them with a handful of coarse salt, and scrub them against themselves, picking them up by the handful and rubbing them together. Do this hard enough to get any and all dirt off, but with a soft enough touch so as not to break the shells. Rinse the clams, soak them in cold water again, and then drain them when the pan is ready for them.

IF YOU HAVEN'T HAD TIME TO GO TO THE HEALTH FOOD OR SPECIALTY STORE...

Your body will thank you if you make the upgrade.

IF YOU DON'T HAVE...	YOU CAN USE...	WHY BOTHER...
Spelt flour (white or whole)	Equal parts unbleached all-purpose flour OR whole wheat flour	Although spelt contains gluten, it's easier to digest than regular wheat flour and is less taxing on the system.
Barley flour	Equal parts unbleached all-purpose flour OR whole wheat flour	Barley flour is derived from barley—which contains each of eight essential amino acids. It's much better than white flour at regulating blood sugar.
Buckwheat flour	Equal parts unbleached all-purpose flour OR whole wheat flour	Buckwheat also contains eight essential amino acids and is a bit of a super food—rich in copper, iron, B vitamins, magnesium, phosperous, zinc, and flavonoids. It lowers cholesterol, blood pressure, and glucose levels, is high in fiber, and doesn't have gluten.
Raw unrefined dark brown sugar	Dark brown sugar	Unrefined sugar is made directly from sugarcane and is an unprocessed product and has antioxidants. Normal supermarket brown sugar is actually just white processed sugar with molasses stirred in for color and flavor.
Grade B real Vermont maple syrup	3 parts honey plus 1 part water OR 1 cup white sugar for every ¾ cup maple syrup	Low on the glycemic index, a great source of manganese and zinc, maple syrup is one of North America's great ingredients. It's always in my kitchen.
Light agave nectar	Equal parts brown rice syrup OR 3 parts honey plus 1 part water	Agave is super low on the glycemic index and has lots of minerals including potassium, magnesium, iron, and calcium.
Soy milk, rice milk, almond milk, hemp milk	Cow's milk	Alternative milks have a variety of health benefits—especially for the lactose intolerant. Rice milk, almond milk, and hemp milk specifically are full of nutrients and are easy to digest.
Turkey, duck, and/or tempeh bacon	Pork bacon	If you aren't into animals of the four-legged variety, but still adore the taste and smell of bacon, it's great to have another option. D'Artagnan duck bacon is out of this world.
Vegenaise	Hellmann's mayonnaise	Vegenaise is one of my favorite things on the planet—you would never know it's not real mayonnaise and you are forgoing all of the cholesterol. I'm not vegan, but I prefer it over mayonnaise every day of the week.

soups

The stove is really the epicenter of my house—
I am never far from it and most of the time there is something atop it,
simmering away for my family. I am constantly thinking about ways to give
my children dishes filled with as much nutritional value as possible and
that's where soup is a real hero. Hearty or light, creamy or chunky, hot or
chilled, soup often offers the best ways to use seasonal, local ingredients—
the options are never-ending. In this chapter you will find nourishing,
simple, healthy ways to turn that trip to the farmers' market into a surefire
way to get kids to eat the bounty that is offered there. (My son may not be
totally convinced on this front, but we'll get there...)

butternut squash soup

ONE COLD WINTER EVENING I dreamed up this velvety squash soup. The garam masala brings a sweet spice that really complements the flavor of the squash. Lovely as a first course with Indian-Spiced Tuna Steaks (page 150) or in little bowls as an after-school warm-up.

1 tablespoon extra virgin olive oil

2 tablespoons unsalted butter

2 large yellow onions, peeled and roughly chopped (about 3 cups)

2 cloves garlic, peeled and minced

1 teaspoon coarse salt

½ teaspoon freshly ground black pepper

½ teaspoon garam masala or your favorite curry powder

1 large butternut squash, peeled, seeded, and diced (about 6 cups of ½-inch pieces)

2 pints Vegetable Stock (page 36), warmed

Heat the olive oil and butter in a soup pot over medium heat. Add the onion and garlic and sauté for about 10 minutes, or until beginning to soften. Add the salt, pepper, and garam masala and cook for another 2 minutes. Add the squash and cook for another 10 minutes, stirring occasionally. Pour the stock into the pot—if it doesn't quite cover the squash, add some boiling water. Bring to a boil, lower to a simmer, and cook until the squash is very tender, about 20 minutes.

Let it cool for at least 15 minutes and then puree it in batches in a blender. Be very careful when blending hot liquids. Start slowly and work in batches if necessary (you don't want the steam to blow the lid off). Pour back into the pot, gently heat, season with salt, and serve.

SERVES: 4 • ACTIVE PREPARATION TIME: ½ hour
TOTAL PREPARATION TIME: 1 hour plus 10 minutes

vegetarian chili

THIS MEAL WAS ONE of the first I devised especially for my children. My daughter is completely vegetarian (she came to this entirely on her own), so protein from beans and other veggie sources are a big part of her life (and therefore mine). I love this chili because apart from the fact that it contains three different types of beans, it easily becomes one of those "dress-up" meals as I call them—a slight adjustment and they transition simply from tasting good to a kid's palate to pleasing an adult's. My kids like this chili with rice, and we grown-ups top it off with a tablespoon of crème fraîche (or yogurt), some chopped scallions and cilantro, and a dash of hot sauce.

2 tablespoons extra virgin olive oil

½ large yellow onion, peeled and finely diced

1 large carrot, peeled and cut into ¼-inch dice

½ large red bell pepper, seeds and ribs removed, cut into ¼-inch dice

2 cloves garlic, peeled and minced

¾ teaspoon mild chili powder

½ teaspoon ground cumin

¼ teaspoon freshly ground black pepper

1 teaspoon chipotle in adobo

1 28-ounce can whole peeled tomatoes with their juice

½ cup de Puy lentils (small, dark French lentils that hold their shape well), rinsed and drained

1 14-ounce can black beans, rinsed and drained

1 14-ounce can kidney beans, rinsed and drained

Big pinch coarse salt

3 tablespoons tomato paste

Heat the olive oil in a medium soup pot over medium heat. Add the onion, carrot, bell pepper, garlic, chili powder, cumin, and black pepper. Cook, stirring, for 15 minutes, or until the vegetables are softened. Add the chipotle and stir to combine.

Turn the heat up to high, add the tomatoes and their juice, crushing them a bit with your wooden spoon, and bring to a boil. Reduce the heat to low and simmer for 40 minutes.

Add the lentils and beans. Fill one 14-ounce can with water and add it to the pot, along with the salt. Bring to a boil, lower the heat, and simmer for 40 minutes.

Stir in the tomato paste and cook for 20 more minutes, or until the lentils are soft and the flavors are melded.

have the kids help This is great to make on the weekend when you may have some extra time. My kids love to participate in the process by rinsing and adding the various kinds of beans, measuring out the spices, and stirring the pot. It keeps in the fridge all week and is great for a super casual dinner or an after-school bite.

SERVES: 4 • ACTIVE PREPARATION TIME: ½ hour
TOTAL PREPARATION TIME: 2 hours

best miso soup

DURING THE STRICT MACROBIOTIC CHAPTER of my life, I ate miso soup every day for breakfast and sometimes with dinner as well. It became one of my real comfort foods. Since it's full of minerals and said to counter radiation and free radicals in the body, I always feel happy when my kids are slurping it out of those giant ceramic spoons. I use white miso when I'm in the mood for a lighter, sweeter version or barley miso when I'm looking for that depth of flavor.

6   cups water (filtered is best)

1   cup dried bonito flakes

3   dried shiitake mushrooms

1   4-inch piece dried wakame seaweed

¼   cup plus 2 tablespoons miso paste

2   cups watercress leaves, washed (optional)

Heat the water in a small soup pot and when bubbles form around the edges, add the bonito. Turn the heat down and simmer for 2 minutes.

Turn off the heat and let the broth sit for 5 minutes. Strain the broth into a clean pot, discarding the bonito. Add the shiitakes and wakame to the broth and simmer over low heat for 20 minutes.

Remove the wakame and mushrooms. Discard the thick stems from the mushrooms, thinly slice the caps, and slip them back into the soup. Chop the wakame into small pieces, discarding any thick piece of stems, and return to the pot.

In a small bowl, combine the miso paste with a bit of the broth and whisk to combine. Pour the mixture back into the pot and let the soup simmer, being careful not to let it boil. If you're using it, add the watercress at the last minute just to wilt it, and serve.

SERVES: 4 • ACTIVE PREPARATION TIME: 10 minutes • TOTAL PREPARATION TIME: ½ hour

You can make the dashi—the bonito, shiitake, and wakame broth—in advance and then add the miso whenever you're ready to eat.

tortilla soup

I FELL IN LOVE with tortilla soup (and all things Tex-Mex) when I was doing a movie called *Flesh and Bone* in Austin, Texas, in 1992 (I was nineteen). As I had a small part in the film, I had a lot of time to discover the wonders of Texan cuisine—huevos rancheros, BBQ brisket—and to firmly fall in love with chiles of every variety. Tortilla soup became the thing I ate the most, a teenager in a hotel room, feeling very comforted by the texture and big flavor of this spicy, hearty soup. It's usually made with chicken but I sought to make a vegetarian version for my daughter and it worked beautifully. If you have a hard time finding the chiles, check out adrianascaravan.com.

2 quarts Vegetable Stock (page 36) or prepared low-sodium vegetable stock

1 bunch fresh cilantro, stems and leaves separated

2 dried medium-sized whole red chiles (preferably New Mexican *guajillo* or cascabel chiles)

5 cloves peeled garlic, 2 crushed and 3 minced

¼ cup plus 1 tablespoon vegetable oil

1 yellow onion, peeled and diced

1 14-ounce can whole peeled tomatoes with their juice

Large pinch coarse salt

¼ teaspoon freshly ground black pepper

1 avocado, peeled, seeded, and diced

2 scallions, finely sliced

Juice of ½ lime

4 high-quality corn tortillas

Heat the vegetable stock over a very low flame in a soup pot with the cilantro stems, one of the chiles, and the crushed garlic.

Meanwhile, toast the other chile over an open flame just until it starts to get fragrant. Roughly chop it, discarding the stem and seeds, and reserve. Heat the 1 tablespoon of vegetable oil over medium-high heat in a medium skillet. Add the onion, minced garlic, and reserved chopped chile. Sauté for about 5 minutes, or until the onion starts to pick up a little color. Add the tomatoes and their juice, salt, and pepper, turn the heat down very low, and let the mixture cook for 40 minutes, or until nearly all of the moisture has evaporated. Stir it occasionally, breaking the tomatoes up a bit as you go.

In a blender, whiz the tomato mixture with a ladleful of stock until smooth. Remove the cilantro stems, chile, and garlic from the stock and add the tomato puree. Stir to combine and then cook over the lowest flame possible for an hour to really let the flavors get to know each other. Season with salt and pepper if necessary.

When you're ready to eat, roughly chop 2 tablespoons of the cilantro leaves and toss with the avocado and scallions in a small bowl and squeeze the lime over the mixture. Cut the tortillas into ½-inch-thick strips. Heat the ¼ cup of vegetable oil over medium-high heat in a skillet and fry the tortillas for about 1½ minutes, or until lightly browned and crisp. Drain the tortilla strips on paper towels.

Ladle the soup into four bowls and distribute the tortillas and avocado mixture on top of each. As you eat, dip the tortillas into the soup, letting them soften, and be sure to get a bit of avocado in each bite.

SERVES: 4 • ACTIVE PREPARATION TIME: ½ hour
TOTAL PREPARATION TIME: 1 hour plus 10 minutes

duck broth with soba

THERE USED TO BE A PLACE on Mercer Street in New York's SoHo called Honmura An. It was a completely unique restaurant in Manhattan at the time, one that introduced me to the virtues of homemade, handmade soba noodles. Whenever I would come home from some far-flung movie location, I would head straight there. It closed when the owner moved back to Japan, leaving us soba lovers lost and forlorn. I haven't learned how to make homemade soba noodles yet, but the organic packaged variety are pretty great and as they are made with buckwheat flour, they are a healthier choice than a white flour noodle. I make this the day after I make the Perfect Roasted Chinese Duck and think about Koichi, the restaurant's welcoming owner.

1 duck carcass (best to make this soup after you make Perfect Roasted Chinese Duck, page 179)

3 star anise

1 cinnamon stick

3 cloves

1 teaspoon black peppercorns

1 bunch fresh cilantro

5 cloves garlic, peeled and crushed

1 2-inch piece ginger, peeled and crushed

1 yellow onion, peeled and roughly chopped

½ pound buckwheat soba noodles

⅓–½ cup barley miso

¼ cup thinly sliced scallions

¼ cup coarsely chopped fresh cilantro leaves

1 small bunch enoki mushrooms or bean sprouts (optional)

In a large stockpot, combine the duck carcass with the star anise, cinnamon, cloves, peppercorns, cilantro stems, garlic, ginger, and onion. Cover with cold water (it should take about 2 quarts), bring to a boil, and lower the heat, skimming off any foam that accumulates. Simmer over a low flame for at least 1 hour, up to 2. Strain the broth into a clean pot and keep it warm while you prepare the soba noodles.

Cook the soba noodles according to the package directions, keeping them on the al dente side. When they're cooked, rinse them immediately with cold water to keep them from getting soggy. Meanwhile, whisk ⅓ cup of the miso with a ladleful of broth in a small bowl and return the mixture to the broth. Taste and repeat with more miso if needed, remembering it's easier to add more than to take it out.

To serve, distribute the soba noodles into four soup bowls. Ladle the broth over them and sprinkle each serving with a tablespoon each of scallions and cilantro and a few enoki mushrooms.

make it kid friendly Once the soba is cooked and rinsed it can be stir-fried with some garlic and Braggs Liquid Aminos or soy sauce for the kids. Add veggies and tofu if desired.

 SERVES: 4 · ACTIVE PREPARATION TIME: 20 minutes · TOTAL PREPARATION TIME: 1½ hours

broccoli & cheese soup ✕

LUCKILY, MY CHILDREN LOVE BROCCOLI, and although we sometimes enter into UN-like negotiations about how many "trees" they need to eat before they can partake of ice cream, it is a vegetable that they tend to embrace. When I want to give it a new look, this soup does just the trick. I like to add a nice strong Stilton to mine (my love for strong cheese is well known and well feared in my house) and my kids love it with Cheddar. You can determine how sharp or mild you want it. Any way you serve it up, it hits the spot.

2 tablespoons extra virgin olive oil

2 cloves garlic, peeled and thinly sliced

1 yellow onion, peeled and roughly diced

2 large stalks broccoli (about 11/3 pounds), cut into small florets

1 quart Vegetable Stock (page 36), Chicken Stock (page 39), or water

½ teaspoon coarse salt

¼ teaspoon freshly ground black pepper, plus more for serving

1 cup arugula (watercress would be good too)

¼–½ cup strong, assertive Stilton, crumbled, for the adults or grated sharp Cheddar for the kids

Your best, highest-quality olive oil, for serving

add potato w/ broc.

Heat the olive oil in a large saucepan over medium heat. Add the garlic and onion and sauté for just a minute, or until fragrant. Add the broccoli and cook for 4 minutes, or until bright green. Add the stock, salt, and pepper, bring to a boil, lower the heat, and cover. Cook for 8 minutes, or until the broccoli is just tender. Pour the soup into a blender and puree with the arugula until quite smooth. Be very careful when blending hot liquids. Start slowly and work in batches if necessary. Pour the soup back into the pot, stir in ¼ cup of the cheese, taste, and add more if you'd like. Serve with extra black pepper and a drizzle of your best olive oil.

SERVES: 4 • ACTIVE PREPARATION TIME: 15 minutes • TOTAL PREPARATION TIME: ½ hour

You can freeze it without the cheese.

cold pea & basil soup

THIS EASY, VELVETY PEA SOUP is bright green and cool, perfect for
a summer's eve. You can gently heat it as well; kids seem to like it warmed
through.

2   tablespoons extra virgin
    olive oil

2   small or 1 large yellow
    onion, peeled and finely
    diced (about 1 cup)

4   cups frozen peas

1   quart Vegetable Stock
    (page 36)

12 fresh large basil leaves,
    10 whole, 2 finely sliced for
    serving

    Coarse salt

    Freshly ground black
    pepper

    Sour cream or your best,
    highest-quality olive oil, for
    serving

Heat the olive oil in a small soup pot over medium heat, add the onion, and
cook until soft, about 10 minutes. Add the peas and stock, bring to a boil,
lower the heat, and simmer for 10 minutes. Remove from the heat and add
the whole basil leaves and salt and pepper to taste. Let the soup cool and
then whiz in a blender until smooth. Cool in the refrigerator for at least
2 hours.

Serve garnished with a spoonful of sour cream and the finely sliced basil.

SERVES: 4 • ACTIVE PREPARATION TIME: 25 minutes
TOTAL PREPARATION TIME: 25 minutes plus at least 2 hours cooling

slow-roasted tomato soup: two ways

WHEN I WAS GROWING UP the tomato soup I had was Campbell's, and how I love it to this day. We used to have it on Sunday evenings with open-faced Cheddar cheese sandwiches. This is how my mother and I remember it, anyway. Bizarrely, my father and brother always fought us on the validity of this story, as if one would hide serving canned soup for dinner... anyway, I boringly digress... I have given the tomato soup of my youth an Italian makeover using the Slow-Roasted Tomatoes I always keep in the fridge. The condensed sweetness of the tomatoes really enriches the flavor and makes it incredibly kid friendly. Version two is the homage to Campbell, whoever he was....

3   tablespoons extra virgin olive oil

2   large cloves garlic, peeled and thinly sliced

4   fresh large basil leaves

2   14-ounce cans whole peeled tomatoes with their juice

16 pieces (8 whole) Slow-Roasted Tomatoes (page 32), roughly chopped

Coarse salt

Freshly ground black pepper

Heat the olive oil in a large heavy pot over medium heat. Add the garlic and cook, stirring, for 2 minutes. Add the basil leaves, tomatoes and their juice, and 1 can's worth of water (swish it around both cans to get out all of the tomato goodness). Bring to a boil, turn the heat to low, and simmer uncovered for 40 minutes. Stir in the slow-roasted tomatoes and season to taste with salt and pepper (about ½ teaspoon salt and ¼ teaspoon of pepper should do).

version one

¼ cup fresh basil leaves
Your best, highest-quality olive oil, for serving

For the first version, simply tear in the basil leaves and serve, drizzling each portion with your very best olive oil and a few extra grinds of black pepper.

version two

1½ cups milk
Your best, highest-quality olive oil, for serving
¼ cup fresh basil leaves, thinly sliced (chiffonade)

For the second version, stir in the milk and whiz the soup in a blender until it's completely smooth.
    Serve each portion with a drizzle of your very best olive oil and a bit of sliced basil.

SERVES: 4 • ACTIVE PREPARATION TIME: 20 minutes • TOTAL PREPARATION TIME: 1 hour

Version one

white bean soup: two ways

WHEN I WAS GROWING UP my father made his living writing, directing, and producing television shows like *The White Shadow* and *St. Elsewhere*. In Studio City, California, very near to the CBS studio where the shows were made, there was a fancy French restaurant called Le Serre where he used to take me when I would visit him at work (and on special occasions). I would always order French onion soup, really for just picking the crispy cheese off of the sides of the pot. I've always loved the idea of French onion soup—the slow-cooked onions, the melted cheese—without actually liking it. I sought to make a vegetarian version with depth and flavor and more of an Italian slant. This simple one-pot soup makes a filling meal, and, just as I did, my kids love the melted, crispy cheese.

3 tablespoons extra virgin olive oil

1 fennel bulb, stems and fronds removed for another use, bulb thinly sliced

1 large yellow onion, peeled and thinly sliced

2 large cloves garlic, peeled and thinly sliced

Pinch red chile flakes

¼ teaspoon dried oregano

¼ teaspoon freshly ground black pepper

2 14-ounce cans cannellini beans, rinsed and drained

2 pints Vegetable Stock (page 36)

Coarse salt

Heat the olive oil in a large heavy soup pot over medium heat. Add the fennel and cook for 10 minutes, stirring occasionally. Add the onion and garlic, turn the heat as low as it can go, and cook for ½ hour, stirring here and there. A little color is okay, but you really want the vegetables to get soft and sweet. Add the chile flakes, oregano, and pepper and cook for a minute. Add the beans and stock, bring to a boil, lower to a simmer, add salt to taste, and let cook on low heat for 1 hour. Proceed with either version.

version one (with kale)

1 bunch kale, stems discarded and leaves torn into bite-sized pieces
Your best, highest-quality olive oil, for serving

Stir in the kale leaves and let cook for 7 minutes, or until just cooked. Ladle into four bowls, drizzle with your very best oil, and serve.

version two (french onion soup style)

8 thin slices baguette, toasted
¾ cup grated Parmesan cheese

Preheat the broiler.

Ladle the soup into four ovenproof bowls. Float two toasts on each bowl and evenly distribute the cheese (yes it's a lot, but this is the time to be generous). Put the bowls under the broiler until the cheese is bubbly, less than a minute.

SERVES: 4 • **ACTIVE PREPARATION TIME:** ½ hour • **TOTAL PREPARATION TIME:** 2 hours

Version one

fish stew

THIS STEW IS BASED ON a recipe in one of my favorite cookbooks, the *River Cafe Cookbook Easy*. I learned a lot about Italian flavors—especially the use of fennel seed as a secret ingredient—by cooking from the books by my friend Ruthie Rogers and her partner, the late, great Rose Gray. I make this easy, hearty fish stew often when friends come over. I'm not a fan of mussels (long story, Biarritz 2006)—but if you are, cut the clams down to a dozen and add a dozen mussels. Serve with bruschetta to sop up the juices.

3 tablespoons olive oil

4 cloves garlic, peeled and thinly sliced

Pinch red chile flakes

Pinch (about ¼ teaspoon) fennel seeds, crushed

8 small new potatoes, peeled, quartered, and steamed for 7 minutes

1 28-ounce can whole peeled tomatoes with juice

Coarse salt

Freshly ground black pepper

⅓ bottle dry white wine

1 pound small clams, well scrubbed

6 heads-on langoustines, tiger prawns, or the biggest shrimp you can find

½ pound halibut or another firm, white fish, cut into 5 or 6 pieces

2 fillets red mullet or another strongly flavored, oily fish (each 4–6 ounces)

1 teaspoon grated peeled ginger

¼ juicy lemon

2 tablespoons chopped fresh parsley

Your best, highest-quality olive oil, for serving

Heat the olive oil in a large heavy pot over medium-high heat with the garlic and cook, stirring, for 2 minutes, being careful not to burn the garlic. Add the chile flakes and fennel and cook for another minute. Add the potatoes, tomatoes, half a tomato can's worth of water, and a large pinch of salt. Bring the mixture to a boil, turn the heat to low, cover it almost completely with a lid (let some steam escape from one side), and simmer for half an hour. Season the mixture to taste with salt and pepper. Add the white wine, turn the heat to high, and boil for 3 minutes. Add the clams, langoustines, and fish and sprinkle the grated ginger into the pot. Cover and cook over high heat for 5 minutes, or until the clams are opened and fish is just cooked through.

To serve, ladle into four bowls. Squeeze the lemon over each portion, sprinkle with parsley, and drizzle a bit of your best olive oil on top. Serve with Bruschetta (page 212).

SERVES: 4 • ACTIVE PREPARATION TIME: ½ hour
TOTAL PREPARATION TIME: a little over 1 hour

gazpacho

I HAD MY FIRST BOWL of gazpacho when I was fifteen in Spain, and the impression it made was a lasting one. My Spanish "Mama Julia" makes a great gazpacho (and everything else for that matter—she'll come up again in this book) and this version recalls hers. At the time I lived in Spain, families went out to work and school in the morning and converged back at the house for lunch, which Julia would make from scratch every day. Even then I remember marveling at her ability to have a busy full-time job and yet come home and prepare a feast for seven during her lunch hour, sit down to eat, and go back out to the office for the rest of the afternoon, returning in the evening to do it again for dinner. For her it was just what was done and she did it with great ease and love. This soup is so fast and easy, no wonder it was a Mama Julia mainstay.

8   ripe vine-ripened tomatoes, peeled and cored

½   English cucumber, peeled, seeded, and roughly chopped (about ⅔ cup), plus more diced for serving

1   red Roasted Bell Pepper (page 31)

⅓   cup peeled and diced red onion (about ½ onion), plus more diced for serving

2   cloves garlic, peeled and minced

2   teaspoons coarse salt

½   teaspoon freshly ground black pepper

1   cup ½-inch bread cubes, cut from day-old sourdough, country bread, ciabatta, or the like

2   teaspoons red wine vinegar

2   tablespoons extra virgin olive oil

1   lime, halved

Croutons, for serving

Combine the tomatoes, cucumber, roasted pepper, red onion, garlic, salt, pepper, bread, vinegar, and olive oil in the blender and whiz away until it's as smooth as you like it. Chill for at least 1 hour before serving. Season to taste with more salt and the juice of the lime—you want enough acid to make it taste bright and fresh, but not lime-y. Serve with croutons, onions, and cucumber.

tip on peeling the tomatoes   Score the bottoms with a sharp paring knife and plunge them in boiling water for thirty seconds. Immediately put the tomatoes into an ice bath. The skins will slip right off. This method is also great for stone fruits like peaches and plums.

 SERVES: 4 • ACTIVE PREPARATION TIME: 20 minutes
TOTAL PREPARATION TIME: 20 minutes plus at least 1 hour cooling

my spanish family Ever since I was a kid I have had a fascination for Spain—I'm not quite sure where it came from. I remember hearing Spanish spoken all around me in both California and New York and always wanting to be a member of that warmhearted, life-loving Latino culture. One day in tenth-grade Spanish class, I heard about an opportunity to live in Spain as an exchange student and I jumped at the chance. From the spring day that I landed in Madrid, Spain—the land, the culture, the food, and mostly the people—has woven itself deeply into my heart and soul. The family that I lived with, the Lazaro family, became my second and very real family—and they are to this day. Julia, the matriarch, taught me so much about the importance of cooking for your loved ones. She continues to encourage and teach me, e-mailing me tips and recipes, much the way my father used to.

corn chowder

I LIKE TO MAKE THIS SOUP during our summers on Long Island, where the corn is abundant and sweet as can be. I love corn so much I tried to grow it one summer in the garden. The raccoons loved it even more. Now I stick to the gorgeous yield of the local farmers.

1½ tablespoons unsalted butter

2 slices turkey bacon, finely diced

2 medium shallots, peeled and finely diced

½ large yellow onion, peeled and finely diced

2 sprigs fresh thyme

1 bay leaf

Kernels from 6 fresh ears of corn, cobs reserved

½ teaspoon coarse salt

¼ teaspoon freshly ground black pepper

2 cups Vegetable Stock (page 36)

1 cup milk

1 tablespoon minced fresh chives, for garnish

1 teaspoon minced fresh tarragon, for garnish

Melt the butter in a heavy soup pot over a medium flame. Add the bacon and cook, stirring, for 4 minutes, or until beginning to brown. Add the shallots, onion, thyme, and bay leaf and cook for 5 minutes, stirring occasionally. Add the corn kernels, salt, and pepper and cook for a minute, stirring everything together. Add the stock, milk, and corn cobs, heat up and bring the soup to a boil. Lower the heat and simmer until the corn is cooked through, about 30 minutes. Remove the cobs, puree a ladleful of soup in the blender, and return it to the pot. Season to taste with salt and pepper and serve, sprinkling each portion with a bit of the chives and tarragon.

note: You could make this with two slices of pork bacon instead of the turkey bacon, in which case you won't need the butter.

make it vegan Substitute olive oil for the butter. Use a half teaspoon of pimenton instead of bacon. Sauté until fragrant. Continue with rest of recipe, and use soy milk instead of regular milk.

SERVES: 4 · ACTIVE PREPARATION TIME: ½ hour · TOTAL PREPARATION TIME: 40 minutes

salads

I was born and spent most of my childhood in Southern California, where the produce was (and still is) from heaven. My mother started taking me to the Santa Monica Farmers' Market (and nearby recycling center) in the 1970s. During the early 1980s I remember greens becoming prominent on our plates and in our kitchen (we actually had a flat of fresh wheatgrass growing and a press right there in the kitchen—thank God my father kept Mallomars in the pantry to even things out). This early exposure to fresh greens and veggies ensured my lifelong love for all things grown out of the ground—and what better way to experience them but in salads, where they remain intact and in the freshest state. For this reason I plant and try to maintain a vegetable patch and take my kids to farmers' markets. When they get to pick the vegetables themselves, they get a lot more excited about eating them.

miso dressing

I LOVE THIS MISO DRESSING. It works on salads, with veggies—even on grilled fish. Incredibly easy, it stores in the fridge for at least a week. I wish I were joking, but if there is a bowl of this dressing around and I am not looking, my son will stick his entire fist in and lick the dressing off as if it were cake batter. At least it's healthy…

⅓ cup peeled and roughly diced Vidalia onion

1 small or ½ large clove garlic, peeled and roughly chopped

¼ cup plus 1 tablespoon white miso

2 tablespoons toasted sesame oil

2 tablespoons plus 1 teaspoon soy sauce

2 tablespoons rice wine vinegar

2 tablespoons mirin

2 tablespoons water

Large pinch coarse salt

A few fresh grinds black pepper

¼ cup plus 1 tablespoon vegetable oil

Blitz everything but the vegetable oil together in a blender until smooth. While the blender is running, slowly stream in the oil. Season to taste with additional salt and pepper if needed.

YIELD: 1¼ cups • ACTIVE & TOTAL PREPARATION TIME: 5 minutes

balsamic & lime vinaigrette

THIS TANGY, SWEET DRESSING adds real zing to any grilled salad. I have never served this without having a friend ask for the recipe!

2 tablespoons balsamic vinegar

2 tablespoons light agave nectar or honey

1 tablespoon fresh lime juice

¼ cup plus 2 tablespoons olive oil

Coarse salt

Freshly ground black pepper

Whisk the vinegar, agave, and lime juice together in a bowl. Slowly whisk in the olive oil, and season to taste with salt and pepper.

YIELD: ½ cup
ACTIVE & TOTAL PREPARATION TIME: less than 5 minutes

standby vinaigrette

THIS BASIC DRESSING WILL NEVER let you down. My dad first gave me the idea of maple syrup in salad dressings—it is a heavenly secret ingredient.

2 teaspoons Dijon mustard

2 teaspoons real Vermont maple syrup

¼ cup red wine vinegar

2 tablespoons vegetable or canola oil

½ cup extra virgin olive oil

Coarse salt

Freshly ground black pepper

Whisk together the mustard, maple syrup, and vinegar. Slowly whisk in the oils, and season to taste with salt and pepper.

YIELD: ¾ cup
ACTIVE & TOTAL PREPARATION TIME: less than 5 minutes

coarse mustard dressing

GRANARY MUSTARD IS A SPECIAL kind of mustard that is coarse and
seedy. I like getting the lovely authentic French brand in the ceramic jar
and using it for a variety of things—fresh bread with roasted turkey and
cornichons—or this dressing. The texture of the mustard seeds really adds
something to a plate of endive. This is inspired by the mustard dressing at
the great restaurant J. Sheekey in London. I used to order their salad of crisp,
buttery endive with mustard dressing every night when coming offstage at
London's Donmar Warehouse in 2002.

3 tablespoons granary
  mustard

1 tablespoon plus 1 teaspoon
  white wine vinegar

Pinch granulated sugar
(shh!)

A few fresh grinds black
pepper

3 tablespoons extra virgin
  olive oil

2 tablespoons vegetable oil

Whisk the mustard, vinegar, sugar, and pepper together in a small bowl.
Slowly whisk in the oils.

YIELD: ½ cup
ACTIVE & TOTAL PREPARATION TIME: less than 5 minutes

chive vinaigrette

THIS VERSATILE DRESSING LIVENS UP any salad. I use it on my niçoise
salad and on beautiful, fresh butter lettuce to accompany roast chicken or fish.

1 teaspoon Dijon mustard

1 teaspoon real Vermont
  maple syrup

2 tablespoons white wine
  vinegar

¼ cup plus 2 tablespoons
  extra virgin olive oil

2 tablespoons finely
  chopped fresh chives

Coarse salt

Freshly ground black
pepper

Whisk together the mustard, maple syrup, and vinegar. Slowly whisk in the
olive oil, fold in the chives, and season to taste with salt and pepper.

YIELD: ½ cup
ACTIVE & TOTAL PREPARATION TIME: 5 minutes

OPPOSITE, FROM TOP TO BOTTOM: Blue Cheese, Miso,
Coarse Mustard, and Chive Vinaigrette dressings

blue cheese dressing

WHEN I WAS A SINGLE GAL in NYC and my parents lived in Westchester, we used to meet almost halfway for dinner at Gus's in Harrison, New York. It is a great bar serving delicious seafood and their salad was my favorite—red wine vinaigrette with big hunks of blue cheese. We were always a blue cheese–loving family and my version, with a creamy base (can't compete with Gus!), is fantastic on a wedge of iceberg lettuce or as a dip. It lasts for a good week in the fridge as well.

⅓ cup sour cream

⅓ cup Vegenaise

½ cup crumbled Gorgonzola cheese (use the *picante* or mountain kind, not the *dulce*)

⅓ cup cold water

1 tablespoon plus 1 teaspoon red wine vinegar

1 large shallot, peeled and thinly sliced *(- chives instead)*

Big pinch coarse salt

A few fresh grinds black pepper

Stir everything together in a small bowl.

YIELD: 1½ cups
ACTIVE & TOTAL PREPARATION TIME: 5 minutes

anchovy vinaigrette

A TWO-MINUTE DRESSING (if that) that adds tremendous flavor to bitter greens. I adore this with escarole, I could eat it as a whole meal. This is my mother's favorite dressing, so I make it all the time for her by special request. I got my deep love of anchovies from her.

6 olive oil-packed Spanish anchovies

2 teaspoons Dijon mustard

2 tablespoons red wine vinegar

⅓ cup extra virgin olive oil
Freshly ground black pepper

Whiz the anchovies, mustard, and vinegar together in a blender, being sure to get the anchovies completely pureed. With the motor on, slowly stream in the olive oil. Season to taste with pepper.

YIELD: ½ cup
ACTIVE & TOTAL PREPARATION TIME: less than 5 minutes

bitter greens salad

FEW THINGS ARE AS HEALTHY for your liver as bitter greens—they support its detoxification—and I love their taste. Living through the less-than-fertile winter is mitigated by these gorgeous greens that grow through the cold in some climate zones, allowing you to have a seasonal salad, even in winter. I like to bundle my kids up and pick ours from our little veggie patch.

1 large head escarole or puntarelle or 2 heads radicchio, washed really well and torn into small pieces

½ cup Anchovy Vinaigrette (page 73)

Put the escarole in a large salad bowl and dress with the vinaigrette.

SERVES: 4 · ACTIVE & TOTAL PREPARATION TIME: 10 minutes

"When we get older, we'll eat dinner together, right?"
—APPLE TO MOSES

endive salad

THE SWEET, COARSE MUSTARD DRESSING is a nice complement to the bitter endive, one of winter's real gifts.

4 small heads endive, leaves separated

Coarse Mustard Dressing (page 71)

Stack the endive leaves, log cabin style, and evenly drizzle the mustard dressing over them.

 SERVES: 4 • ACTIVE & TOTAL PREPARATION TIME: 5 minutes

mizuna, tomato & avocado salad

THIS CRISP SALAD HAS AN ASIAN bent—miso and mizuna, a peppery Japanese leaf, combine beautifully.

4 large handfuls mizuna (totally okay to substitute Boston or butter lettuce that's been roughly torn), washed

1 cup cherry tomatoes, washed and halved

1 avocado, peeled, pitted, and diced

½ cup Miso Dressing (page 68)

1 tablespoon sesame seeds

Put the mizuna on a large serving platter. Scatter the tomatoes and avocado over the mizuna. Drizzle with miso dressing and sprinkle with sesame seeds.

 SERVES: 4 • ACTIVE & TOTAL PREPARATION TIME: 10 minutes

grilled radicchio with gorgonzola

I MAKE THIS SALAD all the time in the summer when my grill is going. With just a brush of olive oil and a nice strong cheese, you have a rich smoky side in minutes.

2 heads radicchio, each cut into 6 wedges through the core

2 tablespoons extra virgin olive oil

¼ teaspoon freshly ground black pepper

½ pound Gorgonzola *picante* cheese

Your best, highest-quality olive oil, for serving

½ lemon, for serving

Preheat the grill over medium/low heat or turn on the broiler if you're working inside.

In a large bowl, gently toss the radicchio with the olive oil to keep each wedge intact. Grill for 5 minutes, turning occasionally, or until starting to brown and soften (keep the heat moderate—you're not looking to char anything). If you're working on an indoor grill, remove the radicchio to a baking sheet, sprinkle with pepper, crumble over the cheese, and stick the sheet under the broiler. If you're working outside, simply close the lid on your grill. Watch closely so the cheese doesn't burn, you just want it to melt and bubble.

Serve, adding a healthy drizzle of your best olive oil and squeezing a bit of lemon juice over the radicchio.

SERVES: 4 • ACTIVE & TOTAL PREPARATION TIME: 10 minutes

the wedge

A DRESSED WEDGE OF ICEBERG lettuce says American summer—I prefer it with blue cheese, but vinaigrette works well if you are not feeling the dairy. I like mine plain, but feel free to dress yours up with sliced super ripe tomatoes or thinly sliced onions. If there is a wedge with blue cheese dressing on a menu anywhere, a Paltrow will be ordering it.

1 head iceberg lettuce, cut into 4 wedges

1 cup Blue Cheese Dressing (page 72)

Dress each wedge with plenty of dressing.

SERVES: 4 • ACTIVE & TOTAL PREPARATION TIME: 5 minutes

marinated gigante bean salad with grilled shrimp & watercress

THIS FILLING SALAD MAKES a great lunch. The giant beans are a delight—and kids think they are out of a fairy tale, they are so massive. The marinating time is key, so make sure you leave ample time to let it sit.

1 24-ounce jar *la granja* beans (huge white butter beans from Navarra, Spain) or two 14-ounce cans butter beans, rinsed and drained

1 large clove garlic, peeled and very thinly sliced

3 scallions, thinly sliced

Freshly ground black pepper

Coarse salt

2 tablespoons of your best, highest-quality olive oil

16 large shrimp (about 1 pound), peeled and deveined

2 tablespoons extra virgin olive oil

2 bunches watercress, cleaned

1 lemon, halved

Combine the beans, garlic, and scallions in a large bowl. Sprinkle with a few grinds of pepper and a large pinch of salt. Drizzle your best olive oil over everything and stir to combine, being careful not to crush the beans. Let the beans rest in the refrigerator, covered, for at least an hour (preferably a few).

When you're ready to eat, coat the shrimp with the extra virgin olive oil and season with a bit of salt and pepper. Grill over high heat for about 1½ minutes a side, or until firm to the touch and just colored.

To serve, distribute the watercress, beans, and warm shrimp on four plates, squeezing a generous amount of lemon over each.

note: If you don't have access to an indoor or outdoor grill, heat a cast-iron pan under the broiler and then broil the shrimp in the smoking hot pan—this will mimic the charred crust you get by grilling and give you the crispy, caramelized edges that perfectly balance the soft beans.

SERVES: 4 as a first course • ACTIVE PREPARATION TIME: 15 minutes
TOTAL PREPARATION TIME: 15 minutes plus at least 1 hour marinating

classic chopped salad

BEING A NATIVE OF SOUTHERN CALIFORNIA, I have a deep love of chopped salads, a dish that is served there often and in many variations. This is a great main-course salad—the bacon and Gorgonzola are super rich and delicious.

6 strips duck bacon (or whatever kind of bacon you love)

3 heads baby gem lettuce, 2 hearts romaine, or 2 heads Boston lettuce, roughly chopped

1 ripe avocado, peeled, pitted, and diced

1 ripe large tomato, seeded and diced

½ cup crumbled Gorgonzola cheese

½ cup Standby Vinaigrette (page 69)

Cook the duck bacon in a frying pan until crispy. Drain on paper towels, cut off and discard the fat if desired, and dice the crispy meat. Lay the lettuce down on a big platter. Scatter the bacon, avocado, tomato, and Gorgonzola over the lettuce in a mix or in rows, whatever you feel like. Dress with the vinaigrette.

SERVES: 4 • ACTIVE & TOTAL PREPARATION TIME: 20 minutes

italian chopped salad

THIS WAS ONE OF THE FIRST salads I made, and I used to serve it up lots. It's fantastic because you can adjust it to include whatever you have in the fridge, or however it suits your fancy.

1 head leafy green lettuce, washed, dried, and torn into small pieces

2 scallions, thinly sliced on the bias

½ cup cherry tomatoes, halved

3 preserved artichoke hearts from your favorite Italian delicatessen, cut into ½-inch dice

4 bocconcini (small balls of mozzarella), cut into ½-inch dice

Large handful of haricots verts (thin green beans), ends trimmed, steamed for 7 minutes, and cut into 1-Inch pieces

1 red Roasted Bell Pepper (page 31), seeded and cut into ½-inch dice

1 tablespoon Dijon mustard

2 teaspoons light agave nectar

5 olive oil–packed anchovies, finely diced

3 tablespoons red wine vinegar

½ cup extra virgin olive oil

Coarse salt

Freshly ground black pepper

Lay the lettuce down on a platter. Scatter the scallions, tomatoes, artichokes, bocconcini, haricots verts, and roasted pepper over the lettuce.

For the dressing, whisk together the mustard, agave, anchovies, and vinegar. Slowly whisk in the olive oil and season to taste with salt and pepper. Drizzle the dressing over the salad and serve.

 SERVES: 4 · ACTIVE & TOTAL PREPARATION TIME: ½ hour

cold niçoise salad

A TRUE CLASSIC. JUST PERFECT. If I am having friends over, often I won't assemble the salad in one bowl. I'll keep each item separate so people can make whatever version of the niçoise suits their eating proclivities. This is a real standby in the summer when we have people over for lunch.

4   6-ounce tuna steaks

2   tablespoons extra virgin olive oil

    Coarse salt

    Freshly ground black pepper

1   dozen small purple or new potatoes

⅓   pound haricots verts (thin green beans) or regular green beans, ends trimmed

2   heads butter or any soft, green lettuce, roughly torn

1   yellow Roasted Bell Pepper (page 31), torn into strips

1   red Roasted Bell Pepper (page 31), torn into strips

1   cup cherry tomatoes, halved (if the tomatoes aren't super, it's best to slow roast them with a spoonful of extra virgin olive oil in a 275°F oven for a few hours)

½   cup niçoise olives

4   organic large eggs, hard-boiled and cut into wedges

1   dozen olive oil–packed Spanish anchovies

    Chive Vinaigrette (page 71)

Preheat the grill over medium-high heat.

Rub the tuna steaks with the olive oil, season generously with salt and pepper, and grill until cooked to your liking (I like mine cooked all the way through). Let the tuna cool for at least 10 minutes before cutting into ½-inch-thick slices. Meanwhile, steam the potatoes for 20 minutes (or until cooked through) and the haricots verts for 7 minutes and let them cool. Cut the potatoes in half.

Arrange the lettuce on a big platter. Lay the haricots verts, peppers, tomatoes, and olives over the lettuce. Arrange the potatoes and eggs around the edge. Lay the slices of tuna on top and crisscross the anchovies over the whole thing. Drizzle with the vinaigrette.

SERVES: 4 • **ACTIVE & TOTAL PREPARATION TIME:** ½ hour

hot niçoise salad

ONE COLD WINTRY DAY IN LONDON, I was dreaming about salad
niçoise—one of my favorites. It didn't seem right to be eating something so
crispy and chilly in the dead of winter, so I devised this hot version. It's a
one-pan dish and an easy cleanup. Perfect for when you are having friends for
Sunday lunch or dinner but you don't have hours to prep.

½ pound green beans, ends
   trimmed

1 cup cherry tomatoes,
   halved

½ cup niçoise olives
   (preferably pitted)

7 tablespoons extra virgin
   olive oil, divided

1 large handful fresh basil
   leaves

1 yellow Roasted Bell Pepper
   (page 31), roughly torn into
   strips

1 red Roasted Bell Pepper
   (page 31), roughly torn into
   strips

1 dozen olive oil-packed
   Spanish anchovies

4 6-ounce tuna steaks

   Coarse salt

   Freshly ground black
   pepper

4 organic large eggs

1 lemon, halved

Preheat the oven to 400°F.

Steam the green beans for 4 minutes. Immediately toss them together
in a large roasting pan with the tomatoes, olives, and 4 tablespoons of the
olive oil, crushing the tomatoes slightly with your hands. Tear in the basil and
push the mixture around the perimeter of the pan. Nestle the peppers and
anchovies in and around the vegetables. Lay the tuna steaks in the middle of
the pan and coat each with ½ tablespoon of olive oil and rub with a generous
amount of salt and pepper. Crack each egg into a small ramekin and tuck
the ramekins into the corners of the pan. Drizzle each egg evenly with the
remaining tablespoon of olive oil and sprinkle with salt and pepper. Stick the
whole thing in the oven for 12 minutes, or until the eggs are just set and the
tuna is cooked through but still moist. Pull the pan out, squeeze lemon over
everything, and serve.

  SERVES: 4 · ACTIVE & TOTAL PREPARATION TIME: 25 minutes

You can arrange the whole thing early in the day and then throw it in the oven right before dinner.

arugula salad with smoked mozzarella & slow-roasted tomato crostini

THIS IS KIND OF a side dish-esque salad. The crostini act as mini pizzas for the kids. I do theirs with regular mozzarella and mine with the smoked variety.

1 dozen thin slices baguette

Extra virgin olive oil

12 thin slices smoked mozzarella

6 halves (3 whole) Slow-Roasted Tomatoes (page 32), each half cut in half, at room temperature

2 cups baby arugula

1 tablespoon highest-quality balsamic vinegar

Coarse salt

Freshly ground black pepper

Preheat the broiler.

Lay the slices of baguette on a cookie sheet and drizzle each with a bit of olive oil. Put a slice of cheese on top of each baguette slice and run under the broiler until the cheese is melted and bubbly (less than a minute). Top each crostini with a piece of tomato. Toss the arugula with a tablespoon of olive oil, the vinegar, and salt and pepper to taste. Put the arugula on a platter and surround with the crostini.

SERVES: 4 • ACTIVE & TOTAL PREPARATION TIME: 10 minutes

lobster club salad

A CHEF FRIEND OF MINE, Maxime, once prepared a salad a bit like this one. I was inspired by him to try my own version. It's pretty decadent—make it for a special summer lunch.

8 slices duck or turkey bacon (or whatever kind of bacon you love)

3 heads baby gem lettuce, 2 hearts romaine, or 2 heads Boston lettuce, roughly torn

1 avocado, peeled, pitted, and diced

2 cups cooked lobster meat (1 medium lobster or 2 lobster tails should do), finely chopped

1 cup small grape tomatoes, halved

½ cup Chive Vinaigrette (page 71)

Cook the duck bacon in a frying pan until crispy. Drain on paper towels, cut off and discard the fat if desired, and dice the crispy meat. Arrange the lettuce on a platter. Nicely arrange the avocado, bacon, lobster, and tomatoes on top (you can do this in rows or an artful scatter kinda thing). Drizzle the vinaigrette over the salad.

note: See note on page 110 for instructions on how to prepare the lobster.

SERVES: 4 · ACTIVE & TOTAL PREPARATION TIME: 20 minutes

panzanella with roasted peppers, tomatoes & basil

WHENEVER I'VE LET GREAT BAKERY bread go stale by accident, I make this salad. The brightness of the tomato, roasted pepper, and basil are really complemented by the texture of the bread.

6 ounces stale country bread, cut into 1-inch cubes (about 4 cups of cubes)

1 yellow Roasted Bell Pepper (page 31), roughly diced

1 red Roasted Bell Pepper (page 31), roughly diced

1½ cups cherry or grape tomatoes, quartered

2 tablespoons red wine vinegar

¼ cup plus 1 tablespoon extra virgin olive oil, plus more for serving

Coarse salt

Freshly ground black pepper

4 olive oil–packed Spanish anchovies, finely chopped

Large handful fresh basil leaves

Combine the bread, peppers, and tomatoes together in a large bowl. Whisk the vinegar, olive oil, salt, pepper, and anchovies together in a small bowl and drizzle over the salad. Tear in the basil, toss everything together with your hands, and let sit for at least 15 minutes before serving. Distribute the panzanella on plates, drizzling each serving with a little extra olive oil.

SERVES: 4 • **ACTIVE PREPARATION TIME:** 15 minutes
TOTAL PREPARATION TIME: ½ hour

my ivy chopped salad

THIS SALAD IS INSPIRED BY the famous grilled vegetable salad at the Ivy restaurant in Los Angeles. This is one of my standbys—I make it for myself when the kids have gone to bed but it's equally good at a lunch party.

2 large beets

3 medium zucchini, sliced lengthwise into ⅓-inch-thick slices

2 fresh ears of corn, shucked

1 bunch scallions, dark green ends discarded

2 6-ounce wild salmon fillets

Extra virgin olive oil

Coarse salt

2 heads butter lettuce, leaves separated, washed and dried, and cut into thick strips

¼ cup fresh basil leaves, roughly torn

½ pint grape tomatoes, quartered

⅓ cup fresh cilantro leaves, roughly chopped

½ cup Balsamic & Lime Vinaigrette (page 69)

1 lime, quartered, for serving

Steam or boil the beets until cooked through, about 30 minutes. Let them sit until cool enough to handle and then peel them and cut into a medium dice. Reserve.

Preheat the grill or grill pan over medium-low heat.

Rub the zucchini, corn, scallions, and salmon with enough olive oil just to coat and sprinkle with salt. Grill the vegetables and fish until everything is nicely browned and cooked through, about 20 minutes. Cut the zucchini and scallions into a medium dice and reserve. Cut the corn off the cob and reserve. Break the salmon into large pieces with your hands and reserve.

Get a nice big platter and lay the lettuce down. Evenly and artfully scatter the basil, tomatoes, beets, corn, zucchini, scallions, and cilantro over the lettuce. Arrange the salmon along the edge of the platter. Drizzle the vinaigrette over the whole thing and serve the lime wedges alongside, encouraging your guests to use them.

SERVES: 4 · ACTIVE & TOTAL PREPARATION TIME: 40 minutes

You can prep all the ingredients ahead of time.

burgers
& sandwiches

My mother says that when she met my father in 1969, he wouldn't eat a green vegetable and wouldn't stray far from a hamburger or hot dog. Although this was a far cry from the adventurous omnivore he became, the truth is, he never met a Hebrew National he didn't like and his love for cooking all started with his grill. His grilling expertise began with the burger and over time gave way to the mastery of delicate grilled fish, marinated chickens, lobsters, and experimentation with different mesquites.

He would buy the premarinated baby back ribs from the HoneyBaked Ham store which came vacuum-packed and in rich barbecue sauce. The whole family would go crazy for these things, which he cooked to the perfect point of tenderness and caramelized crunch. I grew up standing next to him bent over the barbecue outside at our house in Southern California, watching his careful basting and his fury when something stuck to the surface, cursing like a New York truck driver. The recipes in this chapter speak to the soul of my "dad as cook." They are about satisfaction above all else.

tuna & ginger burgers

ONCE ON A FAMILY TRIP to Hawaii we stopped at a roadside restaurant right on the ocean. I fell in love with a creation I had never tried before, the tuna burger. The ones on Maui were done with Japanese-style pickled ginger on top. In this recipe, I put fresh ginger in with the tuna and let them sit overnight to really let the flavors fuse. I love a recipe where you can prepare it all ahead of time and then assemble it quickly just before you eat.

1	teaspoon wasabi powder
2	teaspoons Dijon mustard
1	teaspoon water
½	teaspoon freshly ground black pepper
½	teaspoon coarse salt
1	tablespoon peeled and finely minced fresh ginger
1	tablespoon peeled and finely minced garlic
1½	tablespoons peanut oil, plus more for cooking
1	pound highest-quality tuna, cut into 1-inch pieces
2	tablespoons extra virgin olive oil
3	shallots, peeled and thinly sliced
4	sprouted grain or whole wheat hamburger buns
½	cup Soy & Sesame Mayo (recipe follows)
	Handful fresh arugula

Combine the wasabi, mustard, and water in a small bowl. Scrape it into a food processor along with the pepper, salt, ginger, garlic, and peanut oil. Pulse it all together to make a flavorful paste. Add the tuna and pulse just to combine—be careful not to overprocess the tuna as you want your burgers to have texture. Form the mixture into 4 burgers and set in the refrigerator for at least an hour (up to overnight) to let the flavors really settle in.

Meanwhile, heat the olive oil over medium-high heat in a skillet. Add the shallots and sauté for about 10 minutes, until they get soft and sweet and a little brown. Reserve.

Preheat your grill or grill pan over high heat.

Rub the tuna burgers with a little peanut oil and grill for 2 or 3 minutes a side, to desired doneness. Grill the buns alongside the burgers. Spread the buns with the mayo, pile on the sautéed shallots and a bit of arugula, and tuck in the burgers.

SERVES: 4 · ACTIVE PREPARATION TIME: 15 minutes
TOTAL PREPARATION TIME: 15 minutes plus at least 1 hour chilling

The patties can be formed and refrigerated.

soy & sesame mayo

THIS IS A GOOD TOPPING option for tuna burgers.

½	cup Vegenaise
2	teaspoons soy sauce
2	teaspoons toasted sesame oil

Whisk everything together.

YIELD: ½ cup · ACTIVE & TOTAL PREPARATION TIME: less than 5 minutes

cheesy stuffed burgers

I ORIGINALLY CAME UP WITH the "stuffed" idea when filling a turkey burger with stuffing for a mini Thanksgiving recipe. I thought cheese would work well and, boy, does it. I like it with Gruyère, but kids definitely like something milder. You can use whatever cheese you've got in the fridge. Everyone in my house goes crazy for these things.

1 tablespoon extra virgin olive oil

½ cup peeled and finely minced yellow onion

1 tablespoon very finely chopped fresh rosemary

1 pound ground turkey or ground beef chuck

½ teaspoon coarse salt

¼ teaspoon freshly ground black pepper

½ cup coarsely grated cheese of your choice

4 sprouted grain or whole wheat burger buns

Heat the olive oil in a small skillet over low heat. Add the onion and rosemary and cook for about 10 minutes, or until quite soft and sweet. Let the onion mixture cool a bit and then put it in a large mixing bowl with the turkey, salt, and pepper. Mush the ingredients together with a wooden spoon or with your hands. Divide the mixture into quarters. Divide each quarter in half and form into 2 patties. Place 2 tablespoons of cheese onto one pattie and sandwich with the other, pinching the edges. Repeat this process with the remaining turkey and cheese.

Preheat your grill or broiler to high.

Cook the burgers for 5 minutes on the first side, flip, and cook for 4 more minutes, or until the burgers are browned and firm. Serve them on grilled sprouted grain or whole wheat buns with all of your favorite fixings.

SERVES: 4 • ACTIVE & TOTAL PREPARATION TIME: ½ hour

The patties can be formed and refrigerated.

homemade veggie burgers

AS MY DAUGHTER IS VEGETARIAN, I am always looking for creative ways to feed her. We once bought veggie burgers from a health food store that, upon cooking, became brown, rubbery, and frankly terrifying. Sure that a homemade version could be created, I came up with this easy, super healthy version that Apple asks for weekly. My guys like these with avocado; I add ripe tomato and red onion and even pickled jalapeños to mine.

2 tablespoons extra virgin olive oil

1 small yellow onion, peeled and finely diced

2 cloves garlic, peeled and minced

¼ teaspoon ground cumin

½ teaspoon coarse salt

¼ teaspoon freshly ground black pepper

1 14-ounce can black beans, drained and rinsed

½ cup cooked brown rice

1 tablespoon finely chopped fresh cilantro

2 tablespoons flour

3 tablespoons safflower oil

4 sprouted grain or whole wheat burger buns

Heat the olive oil in a medium sauté pan over medium-low heat. Sauté the onion, garlic, and cumin together until softened and fragrant, about 7 minutes. Add the salt, pepper, beans, and rice and cook, stirring, for 2 minutes. Add the cilantro and mash the mixture with a potato masher just to combine and get some cohesion—you want the burgers to have some texture.

Let the mixture cool until it's easy to handle. Form the mixture into 4 patties. At this point, you can set the burgers in the fridge for a few hours. Dust on both sides with flour. Heat the safflower oil in a large skillet over medium-high heat and brown the burgers on both sides, about a minute on each side. Serve them on grilled sprouted grain or whole wheat buns with all of your favorite fixings.

SERVES: 4 • ACTIVE PREPARATION TIME: 25 minutes
TOTAL PREPARATION TIME: 25 minutes plus at least 10 minutes cooling

portobello & slow-roasted tomato burgers

HERE IS ANOTHER DELICIOUS VEGETARIAN burger option to serve. Portobello mushrooms with their meaty flavor really come alive with the Slow-Roasted Tomatoes and smoked mozzarella combo, but you can dress them up anyway you like. And believe it or not, even kids love them...just feel free to leave out the "mushroom" word.

½ cup extra virgin olive oil, divided

2 cloves garlic, peeled and crushed

Pinch coarse salt

A few fresh grinds black pepper

Juice of 1 lemon

4 large portobello mushrooms

1 sweet yellow onion, peeled and cut into thick slices

4 sprouted grain or whole wheat burger buns

8 halves (4 whole) Slow-Roasted Tomatoes (page 32)

A few slices smoked mozzarella

Small handful fresh arugula or 4 Boston lettuce leaves, for serving

Combine ¼ cup of the olive oil with the garlic, salt, pepper, and lemon juice in a shallow bowl. Cut 3 slits through the top of each mushroom, being sure not to cut all the way through. Coat the mushrooms in the mixture and let them sit for about 15 minutes, being sure to get some of the mixture in the slits.

Heat the grill with a low flame.

Grill the mushrooms, turning occasionally, for 15 minutes, or until softened and a bit browned.

Remove the mushrooms to a baking sheet and preheat the broiler. Turn the grill up to medium high, coat the onion slices with 2 tablespoons of olive oil, and grill for about 2 minutes a side, or until slightly softened and browned. Cut the buns in half and grill alongside if you wish. Drizzle the cut side of the buns with the last 2 tablespoons of olive oil and sprinkle with coarse salt.

Top each mushroom with the slow-roasted tomatoes, grilled onion, and smoked mozzarella. Run under the broiler until just melted and serve in the buns with a bit of arugula.

make it vegan Omit the smoked mozzarella. See page 102 for another vegan version.

SERVES: 4 • **ACTIVE PREPARATION TIME:** 25 minutes • **TOTAL PREPARATION TIME:** 40 minutes

asian portobello burgers

THIS BURGER OF PORTOBELLO MUSHROOM basted with soy sauce and sesame oil is a delicious vegan version. The trick with portobellos is cooking them for a long time over low heat, concentrating their meaty flavor.

2 tablespoons soy sauce

4 portobello mushrooms

½ cup toasted sesame oil

4 brioche or sprouted grain hamburger buns, toasted

½ cup Soy & Sesame Mayo (page 96)

Handful fresh mizuna or arugula

Drizzle the soy sauce on both sides of the mushrooms and then brush each side with sesame oil. Let them sit for at least 10 minutes—this is a good time to preheat the grill over low heat.

Grill the mushrooms, turning occasionally, for 15 minutes, or until softened and a bit browned.

Brush the cut sides of the buns with sesame oil and spread with the mayo. Place the portobellos into the buns along with a few greens.

SERVES: 4 · ACTIVE PREPARATION TIME: 25 minutes · TOTAL PREPARATION TIME: 40 minutes

duck & rosemary burgers with plum ketchup

THIS IS INSPIRED BY the only and best duck burger I ever had at the Melrose Bar and Grill in Los Angeles. I have been known to drive there directly from the airport to have one with fries and a good glass of California pinot noir. The restaurant recently closed, but I rustled this version up in my own kitchen. It's almost as good as the original.

1 pound ground duck breast (if you have a nice butcher, he should be able to do this—it's about 2 regular-sized skinless duck breasts, minced), at room temperature

½ teaspoon coarse salt

¼ teaspoon freshly ground black pepper

1 tablespoon very finely minced fresh rosemary

4 sprouted grain or whole wheat hamburger buns

Plum Ketchup (recipe follows)

Preheat the grill with a medium-high flame.

Thoroughly mix the duck with the salt, pepper, and rosemary. Form the mixture into 4 burgers, each about ¾-inch thick. Grill for 5–6 minutes a side, or until firm to the touch—I like them quite well done, but cook them to your liking. Meanwhile, cut the buns in half and grill them alongside the burgers just until they're golden brown. While the burgers rest, slather the buns with Plum Ketchup, and sandwich in the burgers.

SERVES: 4 • ACTIVE & TOTAL PREPARATION TIME: 15 minutes

 The patties can be formed and refrigerated.

plum ketchup

THIS TAKES TWO SECONDS and really works on duck burgers. It works on turkey burgers too.

¼ cup ketchup

¼ cup plum jam

Stir the ketchup and jam together.

YIELD: ½ cup • ACTIVE & TOTAL PREPARATION TIME: less than 5 minutes

crab cake burgers
with spicy remoulade

ONE DAY MY *SPONGEBOB SQUAREPANTS*—**WATCHING** son asked me what
a krabby pattie was. I gathered that it was a sort of crab cake burger and so I
endeavored to make one. Man, are these things good. I slather them with my
homemade Spicy Remoulade and please a crowd. It's even a hit with kids.

2	tablespoons extra virgin olive oil
2/3	cup peeled and finely diced shallots (about 3 or 4 large shallots)
1	pound jumbo lump crabmeat
2	tablespoons finely chopped fresh parsley
1	lemon, zested and then cut in half
2	medium eggs, beaten together
3/4	cup Vegenaise
	Big pinch coarse salt
	A few fresh grinds black pepper
2	cups fresh bread crumbs
3	tablespoons safflower oil
4	brioche hamburger buns, toasted
	Spicy Remoulade (page 105)

Heat the olive oil in a small frying pan over medium heat. Add the shallots
and cook, stirring, for about 5 minutes, or until just softened. Let the shallots
cool. In a large bowl, using your hands or a wooden spoon, combine the
shallots with the crab, parsley, lemon zest, eggs, Vegenaise, salt, pepper, and
bread crumbs. Form the mixture into 4 patties, wrap each one tightly with
plastic wrap, and set in the fridge for at least 2 hours, up to overnight. When
you're ready to eat, heat the safflower oil over medium-high heat in a large
skillet. Cook the burgers until browned on both sides, about 1½ minutes per
side.

Squeeze a bit of lemon over each burger and serve on the toasted buns
spread generously with Spicy Remoulade.

SERVES: 4 • **ACTIVE PREPARATION TIME:** 25 minutes
TOTAL PREPARATION TIME: 25 minutes plus at least 2 hours chilling

spicy remoulade

THIS TOPPING IS CREAMY, TANGY, and spicy, bringing a zing to seafood. It's also great as a dip for fish fingers.

1	cup Vegenaise
10	cornichons, finely chopped
2	tablespoons peeled and finely chopped white onion
1	teaspoon Lee's Homemade Sriracha (page 35) or commercial sriracha, or to taste
¼	teaspoon freshly ground black pepper
	Juice of ½ lemon

Stir everything together.

YIELD: 1 cup • **ACTIVE & TOTAL PREPARATION TIME:** less than 5 minutes

"Kiddish" food.

—MOSES

grilled tuna rolls

I BASICALLY LOVE ANYTHING that comes in a hot dog bun...except hot dogs (sorry, Dad). I mean, what the heck is in those things? Anyway, inspired by the glorious East Coast tradition of fish deliciousness in a bun, I made these one summer when I had tuna steaks in the fridge for dinner but had an unexpected group of hungry lunch guests. The tuna stretches really far in the hot dog buns and the vinaigrette really makes it pop.

2 tablespoons sweet white miso paste

1 tablespoon vegetable, sunflower, or rice bran oil

1 tablespoon light agave nectar

1 teaspoon water

1 tablespoon rice wine vinegar

Pinch fine salt

2 ½-inch-thick tuna steaks or 1 large tuna steak, cut in half horizontally

2 tablespoons sesame seeds, divided

4 hot dog buns, divided

1 head butter lettuce, leaves separated

¼ cup Shallot & Cilantro Vinaigrette (page 107), for serving

2 tablespoons fresh cilantro leaves, for serving

Preheat the grill or grill pan over high heat.

Whisk together the miso, oil, agave, water, and rice wine vinegar. Season to taste with salt. Rub the tuna steaks all over with the mixture and place on the grill. Evenly sprinkle 1 tablespoon of the sesame seeds on the fish. Grill on the first side for 3 minutes, flip, and sprinkle the cooked sides with the remaining sesame seeds. Grill for an additional 3 minutes and then remove to a plate. I like the tuna to be just cooked through, but feel free to grill for less time if you prefer it medium or even rare.

To serve, grill or toast the buns. Lay a few lettuce leaves on the bottom half of each bun. Cut the tuna into ½-inch slices across the grain and evenly distribute on the lettuce. Drizzle each sandwich with a tablespoon of the vinaigrette, being sure to get plenty of sliced shallots in each spoonful, and sprinkle with the cilantro leaves. Close each sandwich with the top halves of the buns and serve with lots of napkins.

SERVES: 4 · ACTIVE & TOTAL PREPARATION TIME: 20 minutes

shallot & cilantro vinaigrette

2½ tablespoons rice wine
vinegar

1 tablespoon light agave
nectar

1 tablespoon soy sauce

¼ cup vegetable or sunflower
oil

A few dashes hot pepper
sesame oil or your favorite
hot sauce

2 shallots, peeled and very
thinly sliced

1 tablespoon roughly
chopped fresh cilantro

Whisk the vinegar, agave, and soy sauce together. While whisking, drizzle in the vegetable oil. Add the hot pepper sesame oil to taste and stir in the shallots and cilantro. If you make this in advance, be sure to stir it well before serving.

 YIELD: ¾ cup • ACTIVE & TOTAL
PREPARATION TIME: less than 5 minutes

grilled tuna & gruyère sandwiches

WHEN I WAS A TEENAGER growing up in New York City, I spent most of my allowance at two places: an establishment called Jackson Hole (and the other I don't think I can disclose). These are family-owned greasy spoons where we would gather to be taught how to swear in Greek by the borderline-handsome guys who worked there, smoke cigarettes, and, if it was early in the week, eat tuna melts on rye bread. Since my high school days I have been a devotee of the NYC-style tuna melt. For my home version I do them with Gruyère and a country-style bread from the bakery, but anything works. For the kids I use a milder cheese like Swiss or Cheddar. I like to serve with a great potato chip and Bubbies sweet-and-sour pickles.

12 ounces best-quality canned or jarred tuna packed in olive oil

¼ cup plus 2 tablespoons Vegenaise

1 teaspoon Dijon mustard

Large pinch celery seeds

Freshly ground black pepper to taste

8 slices freshly baked country bread

½ cup grated Gruyère cheese

2 tablespoons unsalted butter

Mix the tuna, ¼ cup Vegenaise, mustard, celery seeds, and pepper together in a small bowl. Spread the remaining 2 tablespoons of Vegenaise on 4 slices of the bread. Divide the tuna on these 4 slices and evenly scatter the cheese on top of the tuna. Sandwich with the remaining 4 slices of bread. Melt the butter in your largest nonstick skillet (or in 2 medium skillets) over medium-high heat. Fry the sandwiches for a minute on the first side, or until the bread is golden. Turn the sandwiches, put a lid on the skillet, and cook for an additional minute. Cut each sandwich in half and serve.

SERVES: 4 • ACTIVE & TOTAL PREPARATION TIME: 10 minutes

You can make the tuna salad ahead of time.

turkey BLTs

I GREW UP SPENDING THE SUMMERS in Williamstown, Massachusetts, going to tennis camp while my mother was rehearsing plays at Williamstown Theatre. Every day my father would take my brother and me to the Williams College "commons," now known as the "snack bar." Every day I ate a BLT on that crazily spongy supermarket bread, French fries, and a milk shake. Wow. I haven't lost my love for these incredibly American sandwiches and I make them constantly. I'm not sure how healthy bacon is in general, but I know it's incredibly delicious.

8 slices organic turkey bacon (or whatever kind of bacon you love)

8 slices sprouted grain or whole wheat sandwich bread

½ cup Vegenaise

Coarse salt

Freshly ground black pepper

Handful baby arugula or 4 leaves Boston or romaine lettuce

2 tablespoons extra virgin olive oil

8 halves (4 whole) Slow-Roasted Tomatoes (page 32) or 8 slices fresh ripe tomato

Cook the bacon in a large skillet over medium-high heat until crispy on both sides. Drain on a paper towel and cut each slice in half. Meanwhile, toast the bread.

Spread one side of each slice of bread with 1 tablespoon of Vegenaise. Sprinkle each slice with a tiny pinch of salt and a grind of black pepper. Evenly distribute the arugula on 4 slices of bread, drizzle each with ½ tablespoon of olive oil, and sprinkle with a bit more salt and pepper. Lay 2 tomato halves on top of each heap of arugula, squishing them a bit so that they cover most of the surface. Shingle 4 pieces of turkey bacon on each sandwich (each sandwich is entitled to 2 whole slices). Top each sandwich with the spare piece of Vegenaise-slathered bread, cut in half, and serve.

make it vegan   You can substitute fried tempeh bacon to make a delicious vegan version.

SERVES: 4 • ACTIVE & TOTAL PREPARATION TIME: 15 minutes

lobster rolls

ONE OF MY BEST FRIENDS from my high school days married his beautiful bride in Maine, and we all made the trip up to that gorgeous part of the country. The night we arrived, some of us went to a remote waterside restaurant and ate the best lobster rolls of all time—local eating up there. We were tired from the trip and freezing cold even though it was July (does it ever warm up in Maine?) but those succulent sandwiches and reminiscent laughter left us happy. I have chased that lobster roll ever since. The secret here is the little bit of white miso, which complements the sweetness of the lobster meat.

½ cup Vegenaise

1 teaspoon Dijon mustard

2 teaspoons white miso mixed together with 2 teaspoons boiling water

Pinch coarse salt

A few fresh grinds of black pepper

2 teaspoons finely chopped fresh tarragon (optional)

2 cups lobster meat, roughly chopped

4 top-split hot dog buns, toasted and brushed with 2 tablespoons melted unsalted butter

1 tablespoon minced fresh chives

Whisk together the Vegenaise, mustard, miso mixture, salt, pepper, and tarragon if using. Fold in the lobster meat. Divide the salad evenly into the buns (it's okay if they overflow a bit). Top each sandwich with a sprinkle of chives and serve.

note: One small lobster (about 1¼ pounds) will yield about a cup of meat. I cook my lobsters by boiling them for 9 minutes and then dousing them in cold water to stop the cooking. I use a mallet to crack the shells (much easier than a lobster cracker!).

If you like, make a quick lobster stock with the shells (cover them with water and simmer about 20–25 minutes with a few aromatics like a leek and bay leaf) and store it in the freezer—a luxurious substitute for Fish Stock (page 40) and especially good for a risotto.

 SERVES: 4 generously · ACTIVE & TOTAL PREPARATION TIME: 10 minutes

You can make the lobster salad ahead of time.

playwright's melt

LENNY GERSHE AUTHORED *BUTTERFLIES ARE FREE*, in which my mother first acted on Broadway (in 1969), and for which she won the Tony. He also authored the recipe for this gooey, lovely grilled cheese–type thing that my parents used to make all the time. My mother says that this was a mainstay in our house whenever people stopped by for lunch. Perfect with soup or a salad as well.

¼ cup brine-cured black olives, roughly chopped

4 scallions, finely sliced

⅔ cup packed coarsely grated Cheddar cheese

1 teaspoon curry powder

A few dashes Worcestershire sauce

2 tablespoons Vegenaise

4 English muffins, split and toasted

Mix all the ingredients except the English muffins and spread the mixture evenly on the muffins. Run them under the broiler until browned and bubbling, about a minute.

note: If you don't like the salty pungency of brine-cured black olives, you can make this a bit milder by using what Lenny Gershe traditionally used—a small can of semi-flavorless black olives. A little kitsch never hurt anyone.

SERVES: 4 · ACTIVE & TOTAL PREPARATION TIME: 10 minutes

fried sole sandwiches with spicy mayo & pickles

THESE ARE HEAVEN—FRIED SOLE on a fresh baguette—how can you go wrong? I always make the sandwiches for us and fry the sole in little strips for the kids, the perfect fish finger.

3   fillets Dover sole, rinsed and patted dry with paper towels

1   cup milk

1   cup plain bread crumbs mixed with 1 teaspoon each coarse salt and freshly ground black pepper

¼   cup extra virgin olive oil

1   lemon

Spicy Mayo (recipe follows)

1   baguette, cut in half lengthwise (remove some of the middle if it's a very bready baguette)

1   cup loosely packed baby arugula or shredded romaine lettuce

½   cup bread-and-butter pickle coins

Dip the fish in the milk and then dredge it in the bread crumbs. Meanwhile, heat the olive oil in a large nonstick skillet over medium-high heat. Cook the fish for 2 minutes on each side, in batches if necessary. Drain on paper towels; cut the lemon in half and squeeze the juice from one half over the fish.

While the fish is cooking, slather the mayo on the cut sides of the bread and lay the arugula and pickles evenly on one side. Cut the fish fillets in half lengthwise and evenly layer them on top of the arugula and pickles. Sandwich with the other piece of baguette, cut into quarters, and serve with the remaining half of the lemon cut into wedges.

SERVES: 4 · ACTIVE & TOTAL PREPARATION TIME: 15 minutes

spicy mayo

THIS SPICY MAYO IS REALLY GOOD. I omit the sriracha for the kids.

1   cup Vegenaise

1½   tablespoons ketchup

1½   tablespoons Lee's Homemade Sriracha (page 35)

Mix everything together.

YIELD: 1¼ cups
ACTIVE & TOTAL PREPARATION TIME: less than 5 minutes

vietnamese prawn sandwiches

MARINATING THE PRAWNS (OR SHRIMP) not only packs in the flavor, but it also helps them caramelize as they cook on the grill. The smoky, sweet prawns combined with the tang and spice of the sauces and the crunchy baguette make for an incredible layering of different tastes and textures.

4 large prawns (or jumbo shrimp), 1 large lobster tail, or 1 pound cleaned squid, peeled, deveined, and cut in half lengthwise (butterflied)

2 tablespoons soy sauce

2 tablespoons toasted sesame oil

1 teaspoon peeled and grated ginger

2 small carrots, peeled and coarsely grated

½ teaspoon coarse salt

½ teaspoon granulated sugar

¼ cup rice wine vinegar

½ cup Vegenaise

Lee's Homemade Sriracha (page 35), to taste

Juice of 1 lime

1 baguette, cut in half lengthwise

½ English cucumber, peeled, seeds removed, and cut into matchsticks

Handful fresh cilantro leaves

Handful fresh basil leaves

Put the prawns in a small bowl with the soy sauce, sesame oil, and ginger and stir to combine. Cover and let sit in the refrigerator for at least 1 hour. Combine the carrots, salt, sugar, and vinegar in another small bowl, cover, and let sit in the refrigerator for at least 1 hour. In a third small bowl, combine the Vegenaise, sriracha, and lime juice, cover, and let sit in the refrigerator for at least 1 hour.

Preheat the grill or grill pan over medium-high heat.

Grill the prawns for 2 minutes a side, remove from the heat, and let rest while you grill the baguette halves on all sides until lightly toasted. Slather the cut sides of the baguette with the Vegenaise mixture. Layer the cucumber, pickled carrots, and herbs on one side of the baguette. Cut the prawns on the bias into ½-inch-thick slices and lay them on top of the vegetables and herbs. Sandwich with the other piece of baguette, cut into quarters, and serve.

note: If you don't have access to an indoor or outdoor grill, heat a cast-iron pan under the broiler and then broil the prawns in the smoking hot pan—this will mimic the charred crust you get by grilling.

SERVES: 4 • ACTIVE PREPARATION TIME: 20 minutes
TOTAL PREPARATION TIME: 1 hour and 20 minutes

 You can prepare all the elements ahead of time.

oyster po'boys

MY FATHER WENT TO TULANE University in New Orleans, Louisiana, in the '60s and the stories from that time were legendary. He and his fraternity brothers got into all kinds of mischief including setting up a mini casino in the frat house. With the money they made they switched from beer to liquor. Known to the boys at Sammy (Sigma Alpha Mu) as the cure for all hangovers, the po'boy became their staple diet. When I went to NOLA for the first time when my brother was in attendance at Tulane, my father took me to his favorite po'boy joint with no tables. I'm not sure if it's still standing, but it opened my eyes to the glory of this special, very American sandwich.

2 cups peanut or safflower oil, for frying

1 dozen oysters, shucked (you can get your fishmonger to do this or gently steam them for 5 minutes first to make it easier)

1 cup buttermilk

1 cup plain bread crumbs

Coarse salt

¼ lemon

1 soft baguette, cut in half lengthwise

½ cup Vegenaise

½ cup of your favorite cocktail sauce (preferably with lots of horseradish)

1 cup shredded romaine lettuce

2 very ripe tomatoes, thinly sliced

1 pickle, thinly sliced (optional)

Heat the peanut oil in a deep-fat fryer or large heavy pot to 375°F.

Dip the oysters into the buttermilk and then dredge them in the bread crumbs. Fry for about 25 seconds on each side, or until super crispy and browned. Drain on paper towels and sprinkle each oyster with salt and a tiny bit of lemon juice.

Slather the cut side of one baguette half with Vegenaise and slather the other with cocktail sauce. Evenly distribute the lettuce, tomatoes, and pickle on the bottom half and then top with the oysters. Sandwich with the top half of the baguette, cut into quarters, and serve to lucky friends.

make it vegan   Replace the oysters with similar amounts of tofu or peeled, sliced eggplant. For the eggplant version, the eggplant should be sweated first: slice into ½-inch-thick rounds, place them on paper-towel-lined baking sheets, and scatter Maldon salt on both sides of each slice. Then place more paper towel on top and leave the slices to sweat. After 30 minutes, remove the paper towels, then rinse and dry eggplant slices and cut into cubes. Heat ½-inch of peanut oil in a deep-fat fryer or large, heavy pot over high heat. Lightly dredge the eggplant slices in flour. Add floured eggplant slices in a single layer. Turn heat to medium and cook 1 ½ minutes on both sides. Drain on a paper towel. Repeat in batches as needed.

SERVES: 4 • ACTIVE & TOTAL PREPARATION TIME: 20 minutes

fried clam rolls

I GREW UP GOING TO the island of Nantucket (off the coast of Massachusetts) at the end of every summer. My brother and I were allowed to roam around with other kids and have our first taste of freedom—taking walks and playing in the sun, with the smell of box hedge and salt air on our summer skin. We stayed in a cottage near the harbor and explored the island on mopeds. I usually rode on the back of my mother's moped, and my brother went with my dad. We would find empty beaches and spend the day in the surf, jumping in a nearby freshwater pond before going to our favorite lunch spot, Rhoda's Roadside—a fish shack on the side of the road. The clams were fresh from the island, battered and perfectly fried, topped with homemade tartar sauce, and with French fries on the side. My love for the clam roll was born at Rhoda's. I now make them at home.

2 cups peanut or safflower oil, for frying

4 dozen steamers, shucked, rubbery end discarded

1 cup evaporated milk

1 cup unbleached all-purpose flour

Coarse salt

4 brioche hot dog buns, toasted

½ cup Vegenaise

1 cup Deli Coleslaw (page 201)

Heat the peanut oil in a heavy pot with tall sides until a pinch of flour sizzles upon contact, about 375°F.

Meanwhile, cut each clam in half, submerge it in the evaporated milk, and then dredge it with flour. Carefully slip the clams into the hot oil and cook for about 45 seconds on each side, or until dark golden brown. Be careful, as clams have a lot of moisture that can make the oil pop—the taller the edges on your pot, the safer you'll be. Drain the clams on a paper towel-lined plate and sprinkle with a few pinches of coarse salt. Slather the buns with Vegenaise, evenly distribute the coleslaw in the buns, and then pile them high with fried clams.

SERVES: 4 · ACTIVE & TOTAL PREPARATION TIME: 20 minutes

pastas

When people talk about "family style" food, I always envision a scene out of a Scorcese movie, people delving into a large platter of spaghetti and meatballs and feeling very jovial and happy and yelling over each other. Pasta has become an American comfort food and for good reason: homemade fresh, dried, from the deli freezer—it's got a major ease to deliciousness ratio. When I look at plain pasta I see opportunity, I smell cheese, I dream of the wine that will accompany it. It's easy, it's fast, and it's kind of unbeatable. It's perfect for families; you can always amend the preparation for kids—they are happy with just butter and Parmesan. Many of these sauces are done and ready in the time it takes to boil the water and cook the pasta—just the thing when you come home from work or you've tucked the kids in and you want a quick but really good dinner. While each of the recipes in this section is delicious and dependable, the crown jewel is the Duck Ragu (page 138), a recipe I worked on for years to recall a special night in Tuscany. It brings me back there every time.

A few days after my thirtieth birthday, my father and I took a culinary road trip that started in Umbria and wound its way into Tuscany. We rented a car and began our unique trip, meeting up for lunch with his best friend from Tulane in Pienza, touring the Uffizi before it opened, stopping at any great restaurant, museum, or church along the way. One night the two of us found ourselves in a little town called Cortona. My father wasn't feeling well, but we decided to go to a local village tavern for dinner. Arm in arm we walked up and down hills and over cobblestones in the early autumn air until we got to the old and beautiful restaurant, where we were warmly greeted and given delicious plates of hand-rolled pici with heavenly duck ragu. When I look back at that dinner now I realize that my father, who would die only three days later, set me up for the rest of my life with the wisdom he imparted that night. He talked to me about the importance of knowing who I was, of respecting myself, my drive, my heart. He spoke about his long love for my mother, the importance of the degree of freedom in their marriage—letting the other person breathe while being their biggest supporter. And he spoke of the joy that his children had brought him, saying his only regret in life was not having had more. As we walked back to the hotel that night, I never could have fathomed that it would be our last meal, just the two of us. I thought that he would always be there to guide me, to push me further. The clear love and devotion I felt from him that night has not left me and I suspect it never will.

fresh pasta

MAKING FRESH PASTA IS ONE of the simplest things to do at home—provided you have the right equipment. I kept reading how easy it was to do and then one day I just worked up the courage to try it. The first model of pasta maker I tried was Jamie Oliver's hand-cranked pasta maker, which is great, but then I discovered the electric KitchenAid pasta attachment and I never looked back. My kids LOVE to participate in this project—they hold the pasta up as it's fed through the machine. You can slice the pasta into strips of any width (spaghetti, fettuccine, pappardelle, etc.) or tear the sheets into pieces for a rustic, easy pasta. Also, it's great to make egg white omelets, meringues, angel food cake, or Blueberry Pavlovas (page 258) with all the leftover egg whites.

2 organic large eggs

10 organic large egg yolks

2½ cups 00 pasta flour or 2 cups unbleached all-purpose flour, plus more for kneading and dusting

Whisk together the whole eggs and yolks in a bowl. Put the flour on a large board or in your biggest mixing bowl, make a well in the center, and pour the eggs into the well. Slowly bring in the flour using a fork and then knead by hand just a few times or until a nice dough forms. Add a bit more flour if the dough is very sticky (it's always a little different depending on the size of your eggs, humidity, etc.). Let the dough rest under a tea towel for at least 10 minutes before proceeding.

Now take out your pasta machine. Cut the dough into 8 pieces and roughly form into rectangles. Dust each rectangle with a bit of flour. Starting on the widest setting, put one piece through the machine, dusting with more flour if it's at all sticky. Fold the dough over itself and go through again on the same setting (you are essentially kneading and stretching the dough). Repeat this process on each setting, going from widest to thinnest, until you are left with a long, thin sheet of pasta. Be gentle during the process and be careful not to tear your sheets. Repeat the whole process with all the pieces of dough, laying them on your clean counter as you finish them and covering them with plastic wrap or a barely damp tea towel. Proceed with ravioli or cut the pasta into shapes, tossing it with a bit of flour to keep it from sticking.

SERVES: 4–6 · ACTIVE & TOTAL PREPARATION TIME: *2 hours*

spaghetti alla vongole

SUCH A CLASSIC. IN MY VERSION, the little bit of anchovy, tomato, and fennel seed are key since they add an incredible depth of flavor. You can also serve these clams on their own without the pasta—just be sure to have plenty of good, crusty bread either way to sop up all the delicious juice.

3	tablespoons extra virgin olive oil
2½	cloves garlic, peeled and thinly sliced
	Pinch red chile flakes (use to your liking, the ones I buy in London are particularly spicy, so a little goes a long way)
	Pinch fennel seeds
6	olive oil-packed Spanish anchovies
1	cup cherry tomatoes
¾	cup dry white wine, such as a sauvignon blanc
2	pounds fresh small clams or cockles, rinsed and scrubbed (See Salt Scrubs for Clams, page 43)
6	fresh large basil leaves, roughly chopped
¾	pound (¾ box) spaghetti

Heat the olive oil in a large sauté pan over low heat. Add the garlic, chile flakes, and fennel seeds and cook for just a minute, or until warmed and beginning to soften. Add the anchovies and stir them until they melt into the oil, about a minute. Crush the tomatoes gently by hand, just so that their skins burst and add them to the pan. Cook for about 3 minutes, crushing with the back of your spoon, until the tomatoes begin to break down. Add the wine, turn the heat up, and boil for a minute. Add the clams, cover the pan, and cook until the clams open, about a minute or two. Uncover the pan and lower the heat to simmer to let the sauce reduce until it's thick enough to just coat a spoon (you want it to really stick to the pasta). Turn off the heat and add the basil.

Meanwhile, cook your spaghetti until perfectly al dente. Add it to the pan with the sauce and stir to coat it.

To serve, divide the pasta into four pasta bowls, spooning the clams and all their yummy bits on top of each portion.

SERVES: 4 • ACTIVE & TOTAL PREPARATION TIME: 20 minutes

penne puttanesca

THIS IS REALLY, REALLY GOOD. If young kids are involved, just serve theirs with the tomato sauce. I throw in some olives for my daughter—she loves olives in just about anything. I love this meal because the sauce is done so quickly and has such great flavor.

Coarse salt

¾ pound (¾ box) penne

2 tablespoons extra virgin olive oil

2 cloves garlic, peeled and thinly sliced

Pinch red chile flakes

5 olive oil-packed Spanish anchovies

1 heaping tablespoon salt-packed capers, rinsed

⅓ cup pitted niçoise olives

2 cups Basic Tomato Sauce (page 30)

½ teaspoon freshly ground black pepper, plus more for serving

A few tablespoons pasta water, to thin

¼ cup torn fresh parsley, for garnish

Bring a large pot of water to a rolling boil and salt generously. Drop in the penne. Cook according to package directions.

Meanwhile, put the olive oil in a medium skillet over medium heat and add the garlic and chile flakes. Cook for about 1 minute, adjusting the heat if necessary to avoid burning the garlic. Add the anchovies and stir for another minute, or until they begin to break down. Add the capers and olives, crushing them gently with the back of a wooden spoon, and cook for 1 minute, or until quite fragrant—it should smell divine. Stir in the tomato sauce and black pepper. Turn the heat to high, bring to a boil, and then reduce heat to medium and let it bubble for about 10 minutes, or until quite thickened. The penne should be perfectly cooked at this point. Drain pasta, reserving a few tablespoons of pasta cooking water. Add pasta to the skillet with the sauce and stir to coat, adding a bit of the pasta cooking water if necessary to get the sauce to the right consistency. It shouldn't be too thick, but also not too soupy. Scatter the parsley over the pasta, add a bit more fresh black pepper, and serve.

make it vegan Leave out the anchovies.

 SERVES: 4 · ACTIVE & TOTAL PREPARATION TIME: 15 minutes

You can make the sauce ahead of time.

spaghetti limone parmeggiano

AGAIN, EASY PEASY. NOT ONLY CAN this be made while the pasta is cooking, you have plenty of time to make a lovely salad and assemble a cheese plate for after dinner. Parmesan, lemon, and basil are a threesome made in heaven. The cheesy lemon basil flavors are also very kid friendly.

¾ pound (¾ box) spaghetti

Coarse salt

1 lemon

1½ cups finely grated fresh Parmesan cheese (about 3¼ ounces), plus extra for serving

½ teaspoon freshly ground black pepper

2½ tablespoons extra virgin olive oil

3–5 tablespoons of pasta water, to thin

Handful fresh basil leaves (from 4 leafy stems)

Boil the spaghetti in salted boiling water, according to the package directions.

Meanwhile, using a Microplane, grate the zest from the lemon into a large mixing bowl. Cut the lemon in half and squeeze the juice into the bowl (I like to use the grater as a strainer—one less thing to clean). Add the 1½ cups Parmesan, pepper, and a pinch of salt, and mix in the olive oil to form a wet paste.

When the spaghetti is perfectly cooked, add 2 or 3 tablespoons of the cooking water to the lemon and cheese mixture. Add the spaghetti to the bowl and toss thoroughly, adding another tablespoon or 2 of pasta water if necessary so that the sauce coats each strand. Roughly tear in the basil leaves.

Serve each portion with a sprinkle of coarse salt, a fresh grind of black pepper, and a few gratings of extra Parmesan.

SERVES: 4 · ACTIVE & TOTAL PREPARATION TIME: 15 minutes

whole wheat pasta with purple sprouting broccoli

SOMETIMES I THINK THAT IF I allowed my children to eat pasta every night, they happily would. Occasionally I try to sneak in the whole wheat variety. It works if the sauce has a lot of flavor, like a garlicky pesto, or this one with anchovy and garlic and purple sprouting broccoli. If you can't find it, broccoli rabe is also delish.

Coarse salt

¾ pound (¾ box) whole wheat penne or whatever shape you'd like

1 large bunch purple sprouting broccoli

¼ cup extra virgin olive oil

4 cloves garlic, peeled and thinly sliced

Pinch red chile flakes (optional)

6 or 7 olive oil-packed Spanish anchovies

A few tablespoons pasta water, to thin

Bring a large pot of water to a rolling boil and salt generously. Drop in the pasta.

Bring another pot of water with a steam basket to a boil. Meanwhile, trim off and discard the bottom portions of the broccoli stems. Steam the broccoli for about 6 minutes, or until just beginning to soften. Drain. Roughly chop it into bite-sized pieces.

Heat the olive oil in a large skillet over medium-high heat and add the garlic and chile flakes. Cook for about 30 seconds, adjusting the heat if necessary to avoid burning the garlic. Add the anchovies and stir for another minute, or until they begin to break down. Add the broccoli and sauté for 5-6 minutes, or until just starting to brown.

Drain the pasta and add it to the skillet with the broccoli, stirring to combine. If it's too dry, add a bit of the pasta water to loosen it.

SERVES: 4 · **ACTIVE & TOTAL PREPARATION TIME: 15 minutes**

fried zucchini spaghetti

I CAME UP WITH THIS one evening when I was craving two of my favorite things on earth—fried zucchini and, well, spaghetti! The combo is a delight and my kids love it as well. The zucchini gets all crispy and sweet.

¾ pound (¾ box) spaghetti

Coarse salt

3 zucchini, very thinly sliced (but thicker than paper thin or they will just burn)

1 tablespoon unbleached all-purpose flour

¼ cup plus 2 tablespoons extra virgin olive oil

1 cup finely grated Parmesan cheese, plus extra for serving

¼ cup pasta water, to thin

Freshly ground black pepper

Handful fresh basil leaves (leaves from 5 leafy stems), roughly torn

Boil the spaghetti in salted water until just al dente. Meanwhile, toss the zucchini with the flour. Heat the ¼ cup of olive oil in a large nonstick frying pan over high heat and add as much zucchini as will fit in a single layer. Cook, stirring and flipping occasionally, until well browned and a little crispy, about 4 minutes. Remove the zucchini to a plate and sprinkle with coarse salt. Repeat until you've cooked all of the zucchini.

Meanwhile, whisk the cheese together with the remaining 2 tablespoons of olive oil in a large mixing bowl. Whisk in ¼ cup of the pasta water, adding a bit more if necessary. You want the consistency to be creamy. Drain the spaghetti and add to the bowl with the Parmesan mixture. Toss together, season with salt and pepper, and fold in two-thirds of the fried zucchini and all of the basil.

To serve, portion the pasta into four shallow bowls and evenly distribute the rest of the zucchini on top of each, along with a couple of gratings of Parmesan.

SERVES: 4 · ACTIVE & TOTAL PREPARATION TIME: just shy of ½ hour

turkey bolognese

TWO OF MY PARENTS' CLOSEST FRIENDS are a couple named Robert and Susan DeLaurentis, who lived down the street from us in Santa Monica. Robert and my dad made a film together in the '80s and became lifelong pals, and our families quickly melded together, following suit. Susan is an incredible home cook and makes one of my favorite dishes in life: her pasta with turkey sausage and meatballs. She learned the recipe (originally made with veal, pork, and the like) from Robert's Italian *nonna*, and it is a closely guarded family secret. Susan showed me how to make it, and although I could never expose her recipe, this one has similar flavors and is made with ground turkey instead of meatballs. It's a real family crowd pleaser. Maybe one day I'll get her to give up the secret!

5–6 tablespoons extra virgin olive oil, plus more as needed

¾ pound Italian turkey sausage, cut into 4-inch-long links

1 pound ground turkey (ideal to use dark meat)

Coarse salt

Freshly ground black pepper

2 medium yellow onions, peeled and finely diced (about 2 cups)

3 cloves garlic, peeled and minced

2 28-ounce cans whole peeled tomatoes with their juice

⅓ cup tomato paste

¾ pound (¾ box) rigatoni

Grated Parmesan cheese, for serving

Heat 2–3 tablespoons of the olive oil in a large heavy pan over medium-high heat. Add the sausages and cook, turning them now and then, until browned all over, about 10 minutes. Remove the sausages to a plate and add the ground turkey to the pan along with a healthy pinch of salt and a few fresh grinds of pepper. Cook, stirring here and there, for 10 minutes, or until nicely browned. Remove to a separate plate. Add another 2 or 3 tablespoons of olive oil to the pan and add the onion and garlic. Cook these until softened and just beginning to brown, another solid 10 minutes. Add the tomatoes and their juice along with about ½ cup of water that you've swished in the cans to get all the tomato out of them. Add the ground turkey, stir the sauce well, and nestle the sausages in. Bring the sauce to a boil, season to taste with salt and pepper and turn the heat to low. Cover almost completely with a lid (let the steam escape from one side) and gently simmer for 4 hours (incidentally, this is a great time to use a flame tamer if you have one), adding splashes of water every hour or so if the sauce is at all drying out. Uncover the sauce and stir in the tomato paste, barely cover, and simmer for 1 more hour.

When it's about ready for serving, bring a large pot of water to a rolling boil and salt generously. Drop the rigatoni in and cook according to package directions.

Serve the sauce over the cooked rigatoni with a nice grating of Parmesan on top. Perfect.

SERVES: 4 with enough for leftovers · ACTIVE PREPARATION TIME: 40 minutes
TOTAL PREPARATION TIME: 5 hours

sweet potato ravioli

MAKING RAVIOLI IS A PERFECT SUNDAY project. Kids love getting in there and helping with all of the steps. I always make lots more to freeze—it's a brilliant thing to have on hand for a day when you are short on time and you want a quick, elegant dinner. This recipe calls for a sweet potato filling, but you can do anything you like: pureed spinach with mascarpone, peas and ricotta—it's a great way to get healthy veggies in.

for the pasta

- 1 recipe Fresh Pasta (page 123), in 3-inch-wide sheets

for the filling

- 1 sweet potato, peeled and cut into 8 pieces
- ¼ cup finely grated Parmesan cheese
- 2 tablespoons mascarpone
- Coarse salt
- Freshly ground black pepper
- Freshly ground nutmeg
- 1 organic large egg white, beaten

for finishing

- 4 tablespoons unsalted butter
- 6 fresh large sage leaves, thinly sliced
- Grated Parmesan cheese, for serving

For the pasta, keep the dough sheets covered with a tea towel or plastic wrap while you prepare the filling.

For the filling, steam the sweet potato pieces for 20 minutes, or until cooked through. Mash the sweet potato in a bowl and stir in the cheeses. Season the mixture generously with salt and cautiously with pepper and nutmeg, tasting along the way. Let the mixture cool before proceeding.

To assemble the ravioli, dollop teaspoons of the filling along half the pasta sheets, leaving 2 inches between each spoonful. Using a pastry brush, brush the egg white along the tops and bottoms of the pasta sheets that you've placed filling on and brush between each dollop of filling. Lay the untouched pasta sheets over the filled ones. Using your fingers, seal the edges around each bit of filling, pushing out the air as best you can. Using a paring knife, cut the ravioli into squares. Trim away any extra pasta so that you are left with uniform, neat ravioli. Using your fingers, pinch each ravioli's edges to be sure that they're sealed.

For finishing the ravioli, bring a large pot of salted water to a boil. Cook the ravioli in batches for 2½ minutes, and remove them with a large skimmer to warmed plates. Meanwhile, melt the butter with the sage in a small saucepan over low heat. Spoon the butter over the ravioli, evenly distributing the sage. Scatter as much Parmesan as you'd like over each portion and serve.

SERVES: 8 • **ACTIVE PREPARATION TIME:** 1 hour • **TOTAL PREPARATION TIME:** 1½ hours

artichoke & pine nut pesto

THIS SIMPLE PESTO IS GOOD with spaghetti or you can serve it as a spread—grill some good country bread and spread it on.

1 cup cooked artichoke hearts

⅛ cup raw pine nuts

¼ cup extra virgin olive oil

1 small clove garlic, peeled and minced

⅓ cup finely grated Parmesan cheese

Pinch coarse salt

A few grinds of black pepper

2 teaspoons fresh tarragon leaves, thinly sliced

2-3 teaspoons pasta water, to thin

Pulse the first 7 ingredients together in the food processor. Stir in the tarragon and season to taste with more salt and pepper if needed. When you're serving it, it's good to loosen the mixture with a little pasta cooking water.

 SERVES: 4 · **ACTIVE & TOTAL PREPARATION TIME: 10 minutes**

cavolo nero pesto with penne & peas

THIS PESTO IS PERFECT in the winter, when cavolo nero, which is a dark green leafy vegetable that's very good for you, is in season.

1 bunch cavolo nero or your favorite hearty winter green

10 olive oil–packed Spanish anchovies

1 small clove garlic, peeled and minced

⅓ cup extra virgin olive oil

Freshly ground black pepper

⅓ cup mascarpone

¾ pound (¾ box) penne rigate

1 cup frozen peas

Freshly grated Parmesan cheese, for serving

1 teacup pasta water, to thin

Steam the cavolo nero for 7 minutes. Whiz it together with the anchovies, garlic, olive oil, and pepper in a blender until just smooth. Pour into a bowl and stir in the mascarpone.

Meanwhile, cook the penne according to the package directions, adding the peas during the last 3 minutes of cooking. Reserving a teacup of the cooking water, drain the pasta and peas and combine them with the pesto, thinning with a bit of the water if necessary. Serve with plenty of Parmesan.

SERVES: 4 · **ACTIVE & TOTAL PREPARATION TIME: 15 minutes**

duck ragu

ONE YEAR I WAS GIVEN a birthday present I'll never forget—a cooking lesson from Jamie Oliver. He came over and showed me how to make one of my favorite and most sentimental dishes—duck ragu. His recipe had more of a Moroccan bent with raisins and oranges, and it was magical. Over the years the recipe has become its own thing in my kitchen, but the roasting technique is all Jamie. I think this may just be my favorite recipe in the whole book. The gremolata topping, while optional, takes it to another level.

1 organic large duck, washed and dried (See Salt Scrubs for Poultry, page 43)

3 tablespoons extra virgin olive oil

Coarse salt

Freshly ground black pepper

4 slices duck bacon, finely diced

1 medium yellow onion, peeled and finely diced

2 medium carrots, peeled and finely diced

2 medium stalks celery, finely diced

5 cloves garlic, peeled and minced

2 5-inch sprigs fresh rosemary, stems discarded and leaves finely minced

3 14-ounce cans whole peeled tomatoes with their juice

1 cup Italian red wine

¼ cup plus 2 tablespoons tomato paste

1 pound pappardelle (fresh or dried)

Gremolata Bread Crumbs (page 139) or freshly grated Parmesan cheese, for serving

Preheat the oven to 350°F.

Trim off excess skin from the opening to the duck's cavity and from the back end. Rub the entire duck with 1 tablespoon of olive oil and sprinkle liberally with salt and pepper, inside and out. Roast it for a total of 2 hours, flipping it from its back to its breast (and vice versa) every ½ hour. Let it cool in the pan until you can handle it. Drain off the fat and either discard it or reserve it for another use, such as roasting potatoes.

While the duck is roasting, heat 2 tablespoons of olive oil in a Dutch oven over medium-high heat and add the duck bacon. Cook for 5 minutes, stirring occasionally, or until starting to crisp. Add the onion, carrots, celery, garlic, and rosemary, turn the heat down to low, and cook, stirring occasionally, for 15 minutes, or until softened. Add the tomatoes and their juice and put ½ cup water into one can, swish it around to get all the tomato stuck to the sides, pour into the next can, and repeat again with the third. Add the tomato water to the Dutch oven along with the wine, a good grind of pepper, and a healthy pinch of salt. Bring to a boil and then turn the heat down very low and let simmer for 1 hour and 15 minutes.

After the duck has cooled down a bit, remove and discard the skin and bones and shred the meat. Fold the duck meat into the ragu along with the tomato paste and cook on very low heat, uncovered, for at least 1 hour and up to 4, adding splashes of water if necessary to keep it from drying out (continue to season with salt and pepper as you splash).

To serve, cook the pasta, divide it among bowls, and spoon a generous amount of duck ragu over the pasta. Top with the Gremolata Bread Crumbs or Parmesan.

SERVES: 4–6 • ACTIVE PREPARATION TIME: 50 minutes • TOTAL PREPARATION TIME: 4–5 hours

gremolata bread crumbs

⅔ cup fresh bread crumbs, toasted and coarsely ground

Zest of 2 lemons

1½ tablespoons finely chopped fresh parsley

Small pinch of coarse salt

Toss everything together.

YIELD: 1 cup · ACTIVE & TOTAL PREPARATION TIME: less than 5 minutes

macaroni & cheese (a few ways)

I GREW UP LOOKING FORWARD to the nights we had mac and cheese; my mother would pop the supermarket frozen kind in the toaster oven and the bubbling American cheese would go all brown on top. My brother and I used to fight over the crispy bits. In this more Italian-leaning (and preservative-free) version, the ultimate comfort food gets an elegant makeover. I love to serve this in ramekins for individual portions, adjusting the flavors at the end for each member of my family.

1   pound elbow macaroni (preferably with ridges)

8   ounces mascarpone

Pinch freshly grated nutmeg

1   cup tightly packed grated Parmesan cheese, plus ½ cup for topping

½   cup milk

Coarse salt

Freshly ground black pepper

½   cup plain bread crumbs

2   tablespoons unsalted butter

for variation add one of the following:

1   cup Basic Tomato Sauce (page 30)

1   ball fresh mozzarella, cubed

½   cup crumbled Gorgonzola cheese

½   cup Taleggio cheese, broken into small pieces

Preheat the oven to 400°F and turn it on to convection if that's a possibility.

In a large pot of boiling salted water, cook the macaroni for 2 minutes less than indicated on the package. Meanwhile, stir together the mascarpone, nutmeg, and 1 cup of Parmesan in a small saucepan over a medium flame until the cheeses melt together, about 2 minutes. Stir in the milk and salt and pepper to taste and keep the sauce warm over a low flame. Drain the pasta and combine it with the sauce.

In a small bowl, stir together the remaining ½ cup of Parmesan and the bread crumbs. At this point, you can put the macaroni in a large baking dish, scatter the bread-crumb topping over it, dot it with the butter, and bake it for 15 minutes and it will be great.

Or you can do any of the following variations, which can be done in 4-ounce ramekins to make individual servings:

1 Put a layer of tomato sauce on the bottom of the baking dish, then pour the macaroni over the sauce, sprinkle with the bread crumb mixture, dot with butter, and bake for 15 minutes.

2 Mix the mozzarella with the macaroni before pouring into the baking dish. Top with the bread crumb mixture, dot with butter, and bake for 15 minutes. This is also particularly nice with the tomato sauce base as in number 1, above.

3 After you pour the macaroni into the baking dish, tuck in tiny bits of the crumbled Gorgonzola, sprinkle with the bread crumb mixture, dot with butter, and bake for 15 minutes.

4 After you pour the macaroni into the baking dish, put a layer of Taleggio on top, sprinkle with the bread crumb mixture, dot with butter, and bake for 15 minutes.

SERVES: 4 • ACTIVE PREPARATION TIME: 20 minutes • TOTAL PREPARATION TIME: 35 minutes

The mac and cheese can be made up to the point of baking way in advance.

cacio e pepe

THIS IS ONE OF THOSE DISHES I like to make when I want a meal that is done in the time it takes to cook pasta. When my kids were babies with an early bedtime (before we all started eating together early), I would cut this recipe down and have a quick, cozy meal with a big glass of wine.

¾ pound (¾ box) spaghetti

Coarse salt

2 tablespoons your best, highest-quality olive oil

1½ ounces finely grated Parmesan cheese (about ⅔ cup)

1½ ounces finely grated pecorino cheese (a little less than ⅔ cup)

Freshly ground black pepper

1 teacup pasta water, to thin

Cook the spaghetti in a large pot of salted water until perfectly al dente. Meanwhile, combine the oil, cheeses, and lots of pepper in a large bowl. Drain the spaghetti, reserving a teacup of pasta water, and add about ¼ cup of the pasta water to the cheese mixture. Stir to combine and then add the spaghetti, thinning with a little pasta water only if necessary so that the spaghetti is evenly coated with sauce (there should be just enough sauce to coat it without any excess). Serve each portion with a pinch of coarse salt on top.

SERVES: 4 · ACTIVE & TOTAL PREPARATION TIME: 15 minutes

arugula & tomato pasta

THE ARUGULA THROWN IN at the end gives this pasta dish a bright green addition of flavor and texture and beautifully contrasts the sweet sauce. I originally got this idea from *The River Cafe Cookbook Green*. I like to make this in the summer and serve it with tagliatelle.

2 tablespoons extra virgin olive oil

4 cloves garlic, peeled and thinly sliced

¼ teaspoon red chile flakes

1 teaspoon fennel seeds, crushed with a mallet or mortar and pestle

3 14-ounce cans whole peeled tomatoes with their juice

Coarse salt

Freshly ground black pepper

¾ pound (¾ box) spaghetti, tagliatelle, or Fresh Pasta (page 23)

3 ounces arugula (3 large handfuls)

Grated Parmesan cheese, for serving

Heat the olive oil in a large saucepan over medium-low heat, add the garlic, chile flakes, and fennel, and cook, stirring, for 3 minutes, or until very fragrant. Add the tomatoes and their juice, season with salt and pepper, turn the heat to high, and bring the sauce to a boil. Turn the heat to medium low and let the sauce cook on a low boil for 1 hour.

About 10 minutes before you're ready to eat, boil the spaghetti in salted boiling water. A minute before it's al dente, add the arugula to the pasta pot. Drain the pasta and arugula and toss them with the tomato sauce.

Serve each portion with plenty of grated Parmesan.

SERVES: 4 · ACTIVE PREPARATION TIME: 15 minutes
TOTAL PREPARATION TIME: 1 hour and 15 minutes

main
courses

Around the time my son turned three and a half, we started having early family dinners all together and it quickly became one of the best parts of my life. The meal, acting as a way to bring us all together and hear each other out, is the highlight of my day. I never could have anticipated the genuinely interesting and hilarious insights that would come out of the mouths of the kids, or just the general feeling of closeness and happiness. The other night, my daughter turned to my son and said, "When we get older, we'll eat dinner together, right?" This comment made me realize how important these family meals are to my children too. The food can be as simple as can be, even Chinese takeout—just all of us sitting together without television, BlackBerrys, and the like, is gold. Sometimes we can't pull it off because life gets in the way, but when we can, I always feel tremendous gratitude.

These tried and tested main courses have come out of my kitchen many, many times. We like it simple, we like it rustic, we like it delectable, and, above all, we like it to say home. Some are super simple, some require a bit of time, but none will fail you. There are two basic family friendly categories here that most of the entrées fit into—the prepare ahead option and the quick and delish option.

chicken milanese: four very special ways

CHICKEN MILANESE IS ONE of the most simple, most satisfying dishes. I like to cut my son's chicken into strips and panfry them, squeezing on a bit of lemon at the end for good measure. The four topping options on the following pages are as easy as they are diverse—choose according to your tastes. If you are having a group, you can make all four and serve them in the middle of the table—your guests can choose.

4 skinless, free-range, organic boneless chicken breasts, washed and dried (See Salt Scrubs for Poultry, page 43)

1 cup milk

2 cups plain bread crumbs (Japanese panko makes the crispiest crust) mixed with 1 teaspoon freshly ground pepper and 1 teaspoon coarse salt

½ cup extra virgin olive oil, divided

Place the chicken breasts between two pieces of baking parchment paper. Using a mallet, pound the chicken breasts until they're very, very thin—you should be able to almost see through them—about ⅙-inch thick. Put the milk in a shallow bowl and the bread crumbs on a large plate. Dip each piece of chicken into the milk and then dredge it in the bread crumbs, tapping off the excess. You should have a thin, even coating.

Heat ¼ cup of olive oil in a large nonstick skillet big enough to hold 2 pieces of the chicken in a single layer. Cook for about 4 minutes on the first side, or until evenly browned and crisp. Flip and cook for an additional 2 or 3 minutes, or until the other side is browned and crisp and the chicken is firm to the touch. Wipe out the skillet and repeat with the remaining ¼ cup of olive oil and the remaining 2 pieces of chicken.

Proceed with one of the four variations on pages 148 and 149.

note: You can also remove the tenderloins from the chicken breasts and make "Mini-Milanese" for the kids.

SERVES: 4 · ACTIVE & TOTAL PREPARATION TIME: ½ hour for the chicken plus time for each topping

OPPOSITE: Chicken Milanese with Slow-Roasted Cherry Tomatos & Arugula

SLOW-ROASTED CHERRY TOMATOES & ARUGULA

2 cups cherry tomatoes

2 tablespoons extra virgin olive oil, divided

Coarse salt

2 cups wild arugula

1 tablespoon high-quality balsamic vinegar

ONE OF MY BEST FRIENDS once called me in a panic—she had to cook dinner for her boyfriend and did not know what to make—she had never cooked anything. I described how to prepare the Chicken Milanese and winged this topping—it was a hit. She, and I, make it to this day.

Preheat the oven to 400°F.

Place the tomatoes in a small baking pan and drizzle with 1 tablespoon of the olive oil and a pinch of salt. Roast for 45 minutes, stirring occasionally, until they're split and blistered and super sweet.

While the chicken is cooking, toss the arugula with the remaining tablespoon of olive oil, the vinegar, and a pinch of salt. Fold the tomatoes into the arugula.

Place one piece of chicken on each of four dinner plates and mound a handful of arugula over each piece, making sure everyone gets plenty of tomatoes.

note: It's nice to mix ½ teaspoon of dried oregano into the bread crumbs of the Chicken Milanese recipe for this version.

ACTIVE PREPARATION TIME: 5 minutes (For quicker preparation time, the roasted cherry tomatoes can be made ahead.) • TOTAL PREPARATION TIME: 50 minutes

ENDIVE & GORGONZOLA

2 tablespoons extra virgin olive oil

2 large heads endive, roughly chopped into ½-inch-wide pieces

½ cup crumbled Gorgonzola cheese

THIS TOPPING IS OUT of this world—I would serve it as a side dish with steak if I ate steak. The bitterness of the endive gives way to its hidden sweetness as it cooks and the Gorgonzola...well, need I say more.

Heat the olive oil in a medium skillet over medium-high heat. Add the endive and sauté for 5-7 minutes, or until browned and softened. Pull off the heat and stir in the Gorgonzola.

Place one piece of chicken on each of four dinner plates and divide the endive and Gorgonzola mixture over each piece.

ACTIVE & TOTAL PREPARATION TIME: 10 minutes

MANY HERB SALAD
& DRIED CRANBERRIES

1 tablespoon extra virgin olive oil

¼ cup roughly chopped fresh chives

¼ cup roughly chopped fresh cilantro

2 tablespoons roughly chopped fresh flat leaf parsley

1 tablespoon finely chopped fresh mint

2 tablespoons dried cranberries

Juice of ½ lemon

Coarse salt

I CAME UP WITH THIS near Thanksgiving one year when I had cranberries on my mind. It would also be really good sprinkled with feta or Mexican goat cheese.

Combine the olive oil, herbs, cranberries, and lemon juice together in a small bowl and season with salt.

Place one piece of chicken on each of four dinner plates and divide the herb salad over each piece.

ACTIVE & TOTAL PREPARATION TIME: 10 minutes

TOMATO & AVOCADO SALAD

1 avocado, peeled, seeded, and roughly chopped

1 cup cherry tomatoes, quartered

¼ cup roughly chopped scallions or red onion

1 tablespoon roughly chopped cilantro leaves

1 tablespoon extra virgin olive oil

2 limes

I LIKE THIS VERSION in the summer. For extra taste, add a teaspoon of ground coriander into the bread crumb mixture.

Combine the avocado, tomatoes, scallions, and cilantro in a bowl. Dress with the olive oil and the juice of 1 lime.

Place one piece of chicken on each of four dinner plates and divide the salad over each piece. Quarter the remaining lime and put a piece on each plate for each person to squeeze over the food.

ACTIVE & TOTAL PREPARATION TIME: 10 minutes

indian-spiced tuna steaks

A GRILLED TUNA STEAK with a twist. I love this Indian-inspired spice rub—it definitely livens things up. Served with Raita and Tamarind Chutney, the flavors are complex enough to make things interesting while making kids happy.

2 teaspoons cumin seeds

2 teaspoons fennel seeds

1 teaspoon coarse salt

1 teaspoon freshly ground black pepper

2 tablespoons peeled and finely minced fresh ginger

¼ cup fresh cilantro leaves

¼ cup extra virgin olive oil

4 tuna steaks, each about ¾-inch thick

Raita (page 151)

Tamarind Chutney (page 151)

Combine the cumin and fennel seeds with the salt and pepper and crush them using a mortar and pestle, coffee grinder, or Jamie Oliver's ingenious Flavour Shaker until the seeds are broken but not powdery. Add the ginger and cilantro and crush until a rough paste begins to form. Stir in the olive oil. The mixture should be a bit like pesto. Rub the tuna steaks all over with the mixture and let them sit in the refrigerator for at least 2 hours, up to overnight.

Preheat the grill or grill pan over high heat.

Grill the tuna steaks for about 2 minutes on the first side, or until a spatula slides easily under a steak and the bottom half of it has turned opaque. Flip each steak and cook for an additional minute. Serve with Raita and Tamarind Chutney.

SERVES: 4 · ACTIVE PREPARATION TIME: 20 minutes
TOTAL PREPARATION TIME: 20 minutes plus at least 2 hours marinating

raita

½ large English cucumber, peeled, seeds removed, finely diced (about ¾ cup)

2 tablespoons peeled and finely chopped red onion

1 tablespoon finely sliced fresh mint

½ cup plain yogurt

A few fresh grinds black pepper

Combine all the ingredients in a bowl and stir. Serve with the Indian-Spiced Tuna Steaks.

YIELD: 1 cup · ACTIVE & TOTAL PREPARATION TIME: 10 minutes

tamarind chutney

1 tablespoon vegetable oil

1 teaspoon cumin seeds

1 teaspoon fennel seeds

⅛-¼ teaspoon cayenne pepper (optional, depending on how spicy you like things— ¼ teaspoon has a lot of heat)

1 teaspoon ground ginger

1 generous teaspoon garam masala

Tiny pinch asafetida (optional)

1 cup plus 2 tablespoons water

1 tablespoon tamarind paste

¼ cup unrefined dark brown sugar

2 teaspoons rice wine vinegar

Heat the vegetable oil in a skillet over medium heat. Add the cumin and fennel seeds and stir for 30 seconds. Add the remaining spices and cook, stirring, for a minute. Add the 1 cup of water, tamarind, and sugar and stir or whisk until smooth. Simmer on low for 25 minutes and then stir in the vinegar. Bring it up to a boil, lower the heat, and simmer for another 10–15 minutes, until the sauce has reduced to a slightly thicker consistency.

note: You can lessen the amount of or leave out the cayenne if you are making it for the kids, but they like the sweetness of this chutney.

YIELD: ½ cup · ACTIVE PREPARATION TIME: 10 minutes
TOTAL PREPARATION TIME: 45 minutes

roast chicken, rotisserie style

I GREW UP HAVING AMERICAN rotisserie chicken at the Brentwood Country Mart in Los Angeles—nothing can beat that place. Still, this version helps bring me back to my childhood. Here, as opposed to putting chicken on a turning spit, you rotate the chicken and it self-bastes. I read about this technique in a Joël Robuchon cookbook and adapted it to have an American rotisserie flavor.

1½ tablespoons unsalted butter, room temperature

¾ teaspoon garlic salt

¾ teaspoon sweet paprika

¼ teaspoon freshly ground black pepper

Coarse salt

1 organic whole chicken (3–4 pounds), washed and dried (See Salt Scrubs for Poultry, page 43)

Preheat the oven (preferably a convection oven) to 400°F.

Mix the butter together with the garlic salt, paprika, pepper, and a very large pinch of coarse salt. Gently separate the skin from the breast by inserting your fingers between the skin and breast and breaking the facia. This will lead to crispier skin. Rub the butter all over the chicken, including a bit between the breast and the skin. Tuck the wings underneath the bird and tie one piece of kitchen twine around them to secure them. Tie the legs together with another piece of kitchen twine.

Put the chicken on its side (resting on its thigh and wing) in a large heavy roasting pan and roast for 25 minutes. Turn it onto its other side and sprinkle with a few tablespoons of water. Return the chicken to the oven and roast for an additional 25 minutes. Turn it on its back and roast for 10 minutes. Turn it onto its breast and roast for 10 minutes. Remove the chicken from the oven and let it rest breast side down for at least 15 minutes. Carve and serve.

SERVES: 4 • ACTIVE PREPARATION TIME: 15 minutes • TOTAL PREPARATION TIME: 1½ hours

whole roasted fish with salsa verde

THIS IS AN OLD DINNER party standby—it's super simple and incredibly delicious and is basically foolproof. Served on the bone, it is full of flavor and moisture. I love it with salsa verde, but you can also just dress it with great olive oil and a squeeze of lemon.

1 very fresh whole sea bass or whatever fish is good, fresh, and preferably local (at least 2 pounds), scaled and gutted

1 tablespoon each fresh tarragon, basil, chives, and parsley

1 lemon, cut into thin slices

2 tablespoons extra virgin olive oil

Freshly ground black pepper

Coarse salt

Salsa Verde (page 156), for serving

Preheat the oven to 425°F.

Cut 4 or 5 slits on each side of the fish, about ½ inch into the flesh. Combine the herbs and roughly chop them. Stuff each opening with a slice of lemon and a little bit of the herb mixture. Put any remaining herbs and lemon slices in the cavity of the fish. Lay the fish in a large roasting pan. Drizzle with the olive oil and sprinkle with black pepper and salt. Roast for 30-40 minutes, or until the fish is firm but still moist.

To serve, gently spoon the top fillet off the bone. You can then easily peel the spine off in one piece from the bottom half. Serve with plenty of Salsa Verde.

SERVES: 4 · **ACTIVE PREPARATION TIME:** 10 minutes · **TOTAL PREPARATION TIME:** 45 minutes

The dressed fish can sit in the fridge for a few hours.

salsa verde

THIS IS A HARD RECIPE to write down precisely. My measurements are always a little different and my herbs change frequently, depending on what's growing in my garden and what I'm serving it with. This is my standard salsa verde—heavy on the chives, easy on the parsley, generous, as always, with the anchovies.

6 olive oil-packed Spanish anchovies

1 generous teaspoon Dijon mustard

1 tablespoon red wine vinegar

¼ cup roughly chopped fresh parsley

⅓ cup roughly chopped fresh basil

⅓ cup roughly chopped fresh cilantro

½ cup roughly chopped fresh chives

¼ cup extra virgin olive oil

Freshly ground black pepper

Put the anchovies in a bowl and cut into small pieces with a knife and fork (this saves you a board to wash!). Stir in the mustard and vinegar. Add the herbs, slowly stream in the olive oil, and season with pepper.

 YIELD: a generous ½ cup • ACTIVE & TOTAL PREPARATION TIME: 10 minutes

 Can be made ahead, but it must be eaten on the same day.

best stir-fried chicken

THIS IS A GREAT FAST ENTRÉE. I love making this when I'm in the mood for good Chinese takeaway but don't want to have the MSG. Ready in minutes, it's a real family pleaser—the caramelized, sweet chicken goes down like a treat.

4 skinless, boneless chicken breasts, cut into small (about ¾-inch) cubes

2 tablespoons cornstarch

Coarse salt

Freshly ground black pepper

2 tablespoons vegetable oil

¼ cup peeled and minced garlic

¼ cup peeled and minced ginger

½ cup minced scallions (white and green parts)

Pinch red chile flakes (optional)

½ cup rice wine vinegar

½ cup dark brown sugar (unrefined if possible)

2 tablespoons soy sauce

2 tablespoons coarsely chopped fresh cilantro, for serving

Toss the chicken with the cornstarch, a large pinch of salt, and quite a bit of pepper. Heat the oil in a large nonstick wok over medium-high heat (this is a gentle stir-fry). Add the garlic, ginger, scallions, and chile flakes if using them and cook, stirring, for 1 minute. Add the chicken and cook, stirring occasionally, for 5 minutes. Add the vinegar, sugar, and 5 or 6 grinds of black pepper. Boil on high for 3 minutes, or until the sugar has really caramelized, the vinegar has mellowed a bit, and the whole mixture is dark brown and sticky and lovely. Add the soy sauce, cook for another 30 seconds, and serve immediately, sprinkled with the cilantro.

note: It's especially good with the Fried Rice with Kale & Scallions (page 198).

make it vegan   Replace the chicken with similar amounts of tofu or simply vegetables.

SERVES: 4 • ACTIVE & TOTAL PREPARATION TIME: 15 minutes

chicken & dumplings

THIS IS PROBABLY THE HOMIEST dish in the book. I absolutely love to make this; it's an uncomplicated one-pot dish that you can prepare in the morning and keep on the back of the stove, building deep layers of flavor. The chicken falls off the bone and the biscuitlike dumplings are light and delicious. I was seven when my mother filmed *The Great Santini* in Beaufort, South Carolina— one of the happiest times in my childhood. I spent afternoons running around the marshes and would come home to freshly baked biscuits by Neetha Polite, the lady who was looking after us. The biscuits in the recipe are inspired by her. When I make this, it vanishes—there are never any leftovers.

1 organic whole chicken

Coarse salt

Freshly ground black pepper

1 tablespoon unsalted butter

2 tablespoons extra virgin olive oil

1 stalk celery, roughly chopped

1 large carrot, peeled and roughly chopped

1 small leek, roughly chopped

1 slice duck bacon, finely diced

1 dried bay leaf

1 teaspoon fresh thyme leaves

½ cup white wine

2 cups Vegetable Stock (page 36) or Chicken Stock (page 39)

2 cups water

1 cup unbleached all-purpose or white spelt flour

1 tablespoon baking powder

½ cup plus 1 teaspoon half-and-half

½ teaspoon fine salt

Fresh parsley, for garnish

Preheat the oven to 400°F.

Wash and dry the chicken (See Salt Scrubs for Poultry, page 43). Discard the back and cut the chicken into 10 pieces.

Aggressively season the chicken pieces with coarse salt and pepper. Heat the butter and olive oil in the largest, widest oven-safe pot you have (at least 12 inches in diameter, with a lid) over medium-high heat. Thoroughly brown the chicken pieces, in batches if necessary (7–8 minutes per side), and remove to a plate, leaving the fat in the pot. Add the vegetables, duck bacon, bay leaf, and thyme to the pot and cook for 15 minutes over medium-low heat. Return the chicken to the pot. Add the white wine, bring to a boil, and cook for 2 minutes. Add the stock and water, bring to a boil, and season to taste with salt and pepper. Turn off the heat, cover the pot with a circle of parchment paper, and put the lid on top. Cook the chicken in a 400°F oven for 1½ hours.

Meanwhile, combine the flour, baking powder, half-and-half, and fine salt together in a bowl. Take the pot out of the oven, discard the parchment, and scoop large spoonfuls of the dumpling mixture on top of the chicken mixture—you should end up with about 10 dumplings. Cover the pot and put back in the oven for 10 minutes. Sprinkle with parsley and a bit more ground black pepper. Serve immediately, being sure to spoon plenty of the juices over each portion.

 SERVES: 4 • ACTIVE PREPARATION TIME: 1 hour
TOTAL PREPARATION TIME: 2½ hours

This can be made ahead up until the point of the dumplings.

fried flounder
with tartar sauce

WHILE I WAS GROWING UP my mom had a few dinner specialties in high rotation. This was my favorite of the bunch—crispy fried flounder. She used to serve it with Stouffer's macaroni and cheese, which I've omitted here (but you could try the Macaroni & Cheese recipe on page 141 to go with it if you want). To this day, fried flounder says home to me. My kids love it just as much as I do.

4 large flounder or any flat white fish fillets

½ cup milk

2 cups fine plain bread crumbs

Safflower or peanut oil, for frying

Fine salt

1 lemon, cut into wedges, for serving

Tartar Sauce (recipe follows), for serving

Dip the fish in the milk and then lightly dredge in bread crumbs. Place a large nonstick skillet over medium-high heat and fill with ¼ inch of safflower oil (about ¾ cup). When a small pinch of bread crumbs sizzles immediately, gently lay the fish in the skillet (do this in batches if necessary). Fry for about 3 minutes per side, or until golden brown and crispy. Drain on paper towels and sprinkle with a pinch of salt. Serve with lemon wedges and tartar sauce.

make it kid friendly Cut the fillets into fish fingers before frying for the kids.

SERVES: 4 · ACTIVE & TOTAL PREPARATION TIME: 15 minutes

tartar sauce

1¼ cups Vegenaise

3 tablespoons salt-packed capers, rinsed and drained

¼ cup cornichons, very finely chopped

¼ cup fresh basil leaves, finely chopped

2 tablespoons finely chopped fresh chives

1 teaspoon lemon juice

¼ teaspoon freshly ground black pepper

Stir everything together.

YIELD: 1⅓ cups
ACTIVE & TOTAL PREPARATION TIME: 10 minutes

salmon with ginger preserves & thyme

THIS WAS A BRUCE PALTROW summer barbecue special. He had a big Weber grill that sat on an expansive wooden deck overlooking Lake Waccabuc. Taking great pleasure in firing it up, he was very specific about his mesquite and the coal he used to get the fire going ("No lighter fluid, it ruins the taste!"). The ginger preserves caramelize on the salmon—it's got a sweet, smoky flavor on the grill. I like to grill slices of oil-brushed Vidalia onions to serve on the side.

4   6-ounce salmon fillets
     (with the skin on)

     Coarse salt

     Freshly ground black
     pepper

½   cup ginger preserves (I like
     the Wilkin & Sons brand.)

1   tablespoon fresh thyme
     leaves

Heat the grill over medium-high heat.

Sprinkle each piece of salmon with salt and pepper and then evenly distribute the ginger preserves, being sure to coat not only the tops of the fillets but also the sides. Sprinkle the top of each fillet with the thyme leaves.

Place the salmon skin side down on the grill, cover, and cook for 10 minutes. Slide a large, sturdy spatula in between the skin and the flesh of each fillet and carefully lift the fillets off the skin—this should happen pretty easily. Discard the salmon skin.

SERVES: 4 • ACTIVE PREPARATION TIME: 5 minutes • TOTAL PREPARATION TIME: 15 minutes

sole à la grenobloise

ONE EVENING OUT AT THE BEACH my mother invited some of her friends over and I was assigned chef duties with not a lot of time to prepare. I made this flavorful, light sautéed fish, based on the classic French preparation. I didn't let her down! The browned butter and fresh lemon are the perfect complement for white flaky sole.

½ cup milk

1 cup unbleached all-purpose flour seasoned with a large pinch of salt and a few fresh grinds of black pepper

4 fillets of sole, skin removed (each should weigh about 4 ounces)

¼ cup extra virgin olive oil

4 tablespoons unsalted butter, divided

2 tablespoons salt-packed capers, rinsed and drained

1 lemon, skin and pith discarded, cut into thin circles

Maldon sea salt

Put the milk and flour in separate shallow bowls. Dip the fillets in the milk and then lightly dredge in the flour. Heat the olive oil and 2 tablespoons of the butter in a large nonstick skillet over medium-high heat. Gently lay the fillets down in the skillet and cook for 2 minutes on each side, or until cooked through and nicely golden brown. Do this in batches if necessary.

While the fish is cooking, heat the remaining 2 tablespoons of butter in a small saucepan over medium-high heat. When it's just beginning to brown and the surface is foamy, about 1½ minutes, swirl in the capers and remove from the heat. Add the lemon circles.

Transfer the fish fillets to a serving plate, spoon over the sauce, being sure to evenly distribute the capers and lemon. Sprinkle each fillet with a bit of coarse salt and serve.

SERVES: 4 · ACTIVE & TOTAL PREPARATION TIME: 20 minutes

fish tacos

THE PERFECT FAMILY MEAL! I like to put the various accoutrements in little bowls so that everyone can assemble their own taco—it becomes a fun, creative project, and a delicious one at that. My veggie daughter omits the fish and has black beans in her tortilla with the salsa and guacamole.

To make it a healthier option, marinate the fish in olive oil, lots of lime juice, salt, pepper, and roughly chopped cilantro (optional) for at least an hour and up to overnight. Grill the fish for a few minutes per side, depending on the thickness.

Safflower or peanut oil, for frying

1 cup unbleached all-purpose flour

1 cup beer

Coarse salt

¼ teaspoon freshly ground pepper

1½ pounds white fish fillets (cod, pollock, and haddock are all good choices—whatever's best that day), cut into finger-sized pieces (about 2 inches long and ½-inch thick)

Corn tortillas

Lime Crema (page 167)

Pico de Gallo (page 166)

Salted Cabbage (page 166)

Guacamole (page 166)

Cholula hot sauce

Pour 2 inches of safflower oil in a large pot or fill your deep-fat fryer. Heat to 350°F.

Meanwhile, combine the flour, beer, a pinch of salt, and the pepper together in a large bowl. Dredge the fish in the batter and gently place in the hot oil, being careful not to crowd the pot. Fry for 3–4 minutes, turning here and there, until nicely browned. Remove to a paper towel–lined plate, sprinkle with a little salt, and repeat with as many batches as necessary until you've cooked all your fish.

To serve, warm the corn tortillas on both sides in a skillet with just a bit of oil or butter. Serve a stack of them alongside all your fillings. To assemble, spread a spoonful of lime crema on a tortilla, lay 2 or 3 pieces of fried fish on top, scatter generously with pico de gallo, a bit of salted cabbage, and some guacamole. I like mine with Cholula hot sauce too.

SERVES: 4 • ACTIVE & TOTAL PREPARATION TIME: 25 minutes

pico de gallo

1 pint grape tomatoes,
quartered

½ small red onion, peeled
and very finely diced

2 tablespoons finely
chopped fresh cilantro

Maldon sea salt

1 lime

Combine the tomatoes, onion, and cilantro in a bowl. Season to taste with salt and lime juice.

YIELD: 2 cups • ACTIVE & TOTAL PREPARATION TIME: 10 minutes

salted cabbage

½ very small green cabbage,
coarsely grated

Juice of ½ lime

Pinch Maldon sea salt

Combine everything together and let it sit for 20 minutes. The cabbage will wilt slightly, but will retain its crunch.

YIELD: 1 cup • ACTIVE PREPARATION TIME: 5 minutes
TOTAL PREPARATION TIME: 25 minutes

guacamole

2 ripe avocados

2 tablespoons peeled and
minced white onion

3 tablespoons roughly
chopped fresh cilantro

1 lime

Coarse salt

Cut the avocados in half, remove and reserve the pits, and score the flesh inside of the shells. Scoop the avocado into a mixing bowl and mash gently with a fork—you don't want it to be completely smooth. Stir in the onion and cilantro. Cut the lime in half and squeeze in enough juice to taste. Season the guacamole with salt and either serve immediately or stick the pits in to keep it from browning (remove the pits before serving).

YIELD: 1½ cups • ACTIVE & TOTAL PREPARATION TIME: 10 minutes

lime crema

½ cup Vegenaise

1 tablespoon fresh lime juice

Coarse salt

Stir together the Vegenaise and lime juice and season with salt.

YIELD: ½ cup • ACTIVE & TOTAL PREPARATION TIME: 1 minute

seafood paella, spanish mama style

WHILE I WAS IN SPAIN as a teenager living with my Spanish "mama"
Julia and her family, we used to go to their farm on weekends in the heart
of Castilla-La Mancha. Julia gave me my first taste of paella—which doesn't
resemble any "paella" I've ever had outside of Spain. She made hers over an
open fire in an age-old iron paella pan. It was the best thing I had ever eaten. I
asked her to teach me how she does it and have made it many times since. This
stovetop version is the real deal.

4 cups Fish Stock (page 40)

2 teaspoons sweet pimenton

Coarse salt

¼ cup good Spanish extra
virgin olive oil, plus more if
needed

6 large prawns, heads and
shells on

2 small lobsters, split in half
lengthwise (cut through the
eyes first—the quickest,
supposedly most humane
way to kill a lobster)

1½ large yellow onions, peeled
and diced (about 2 cups)

1 red bell pepper, seeds and
stem removed, cut into
1-inch pieces

3 cloves garlic, peeled and
minced

2 cups Bomba rice (I strongly
recommend using Bomba
rice if you can find it, but
short-grain white rice will
work just fine too.)

1 dozen small clams,
scrubbed (See Salt Scrubs
for Clams, page 43)

2 fillets flat white fish (such
as sole), cut into 2-inch-
wide pieces

2 tablespoons roughly
chopped fresh parsley

2 lemons, cut into wedges,
for serving

Combine the fish stock, pimenton, and salt to taste in a soup pot and keep
warm over a low flame. Meanwhile, heat the olive oil until nearly smoking
in a 16-inch paella pan set on a barbecue or paella burner, or straddling
2 burners. Add the prawns and cook, flipping occasionally, for 6–7 minutes,
or until a bit browned. Remove to a plate and then add the lobsters to the
pan shell side down and cook for 4½ minutes, flip, and cook for another
4½ minutes. Put the lobsters on the plate with the prawns. If the pan is a bit
dry, add a few more tablespoons of olive oil. Turn the heat down to medium,
add the onions, pepper, and garlic and cook, stirring, for about 10 minutes,
or until just softened. Pour the rice in the pan in an even cross (this is the
way I was taught and I don't mess with tradition) and then stir to combine
with the vegetables. Add the stock, bring to a boil, and then lower the heat
to a simmer and cook for 10 minutes. Arrange the prawns, lobsters, clams,
and fish on top of the rice, cover with a large piece of tinfoil, and cook for
10 minutes. Remove the tinfoil and cook for 5 more minutes. The clams
should be open and the rice should be cooked through. You might start
to hear a crackling sound—this is a good thing, it means you're forming a
crust at the bottom of the pan (the *soccarat*), which distinguishes all great
paellas. Remove the pan from the heat source, cover with your piece of large
tinfoil, and let it sit undisturbed for 15 minutes before serving, sprinkled with
parsley.

Bring the pan to the table, scoop plenty of everything onto everyone's
plates, and encourage your guests to squeeze lots of lemon on their dinner.

SERVES: 1 if you're me, but actually 4–6
ACTIVE PREPARATION TIME: 40 minutes
TOTAL PREPARATION TIME: a little over 1 hour

vegetable paella

WHEN I HAVE VEGETARIAN OR VEGAN friends coming for a festive meal
and I imagine they are tired of being served pasta with tomato sauce at a
dinner party, I like to mix things up with paella. You can improvise this recipe
by adding other vegetables, but make sure you taste the broth along the way to
ensure it has a lot of flavor and is well seasoned.

1 quart Vegetable Stock
(page 36)

2 dried shiitake or porcini
mushrooms

10 cloves of garlic, 4 crushed
and 6 minced

Large pinch saffron

½ teaspoon sweet pimenton

Coarse salt

Freshly ground black
pepper

1 large eggplant cut into
⅓-inch-thick slices, ends
discarded

½ cup olive oil

1 yellow onion, finely diced

1 large tomato

2 red peppers, seeds and
stem removed, cut into
1-inch pieces

2 cups Bomba rice (I strongly
recommend using Bomba
rice if you can find it, but
short-grain white rice will
work just fine too.)

8 small artichokes, trimmed
and steamed for 20
minutes, cut in half and
chokes discarded

1 cup frozen peas

3 lemons, 2 cut into wedges

Quick Pimenton Aioli
(page 173)

Combine the stock with the mushrooms and the 4 cloves of crushed garlic
in a large saucepan and boil over high heat for 10 minutes. Lower the heat,
add the saffron and pimenton, and simmer for an additional 10 minutes to
thoroughly combine the flavors. The secret to this recipe is a well-seasoned
broth, so season to taste with salt and pepper and more saffron and/or
pimenton if necessary. Keep warm over a low flame.

Meanwhile, prepare the eggplant. Sprinkle both sides of the eggplant
slices with a bit of salt and lay them between sheets of paper towels for at
least 15 minutes. Cut the eggplant into 1-inch pieces. Heat ¼ cup of olive oil
in a large sauté pan set over medium heat and cook 2 cloves of the minced
garlic until fragrant, about a minute. Add the pieces of eggplant to the
pan and cook for 12–15 minutes, stirring now and then, until browned and
softened. Set aside.

Meanwhile, heat ¼ cup of the olive oil in a 16–18-inch paella pan over
high heat until just beginning to smoke. Turn the heat down to medium, add
the onion and the 4 remaining cloves of minced garlic, and cook, stirring,
until just beginning to soften, about 5 minutes. Coarsely grate in the tomato,
discarding the skin. Stir together and cook for another 2 minutes. Add the
peppers and continue to cook the vegetables together until softened, another
10 minutes. Stir in the cooked eggplant. At this point the vegetable mixture
can be set aside for up to 2 hours or refrigerated overnight.

When you're ready to roll, place the paella pan with the vegetables
over high heat and pour the rice into the pan in an even cross (this how
I was taught). Add the stock and stir to combine everything. Bring to a boil
and then lower the heat to a simmer. Arrange the artichokes and peas on
top and simmer until the rice is cooked through, about 35 minutes. Remove
the pan from the heat source, cover with a large piece of tinfoil and let it sit
undisturbed for 15 minutes. Alternatively you can cook the paella outside
over a not-too-hot barbecue. Squeeze the juice of the lemon over the platter.
Serve with lemon wedges and the Quick Pimenton Aioli, which is great for
artichoke dipping.

SERVES: 6 • ACTIVE PREPARATION TIME: 1 hour **• TOTAL PREPARATION TIME:** 1½ hours

quick pimenton aioli

½ cup Vegenaise (or your favorite mayonnaise)

1 small clove garlic, finely minced or grated

¼ teaspoon pimenton

½ teaspoon fresh lemon juice

Coarse salt

Freshly ground black pepper

Whisk everything together, adding more of any ingredient to suit your taste.

 YIELD: ½ cup • **ACTIVE & TOTAL PREPARATION TIME:** 10 minutes

wood oven pizzas

WE'VE GOT A WOOD-BURNING pizza oven in the garden—a luxury, I know, but it's one of the best investments I've ever made. Homemade pizza is not only incredibly delicious, but it is an opportunity for a real family activity—and it's fun! My kids love to assemble their own versions—my daughter likes sauce and olives, my son likes a classic margarita. I love four-cheese (mozzarella, Parmesan, Gorgonzola, and fontina with a splash of truffle oil) or a pissaladière (slowly cooked onions, garlic, anchovies, and black olives). As long as you're making homemade dough, you can't go wrong. And this works really well in a conventional oven with a pizza stone—just set your oven as high as it will go and let the stone get all the way up to temperature before you put your first pizza in.

for the dough

2¼ cups warm water, divided

2 tablespoons granulated sugar

3 packages or 2 tablespoons plus ¾ teaspoon active dry yeast

About 5 cups King Arthur bread flour, divided, plus more for kneading and dusting

1½ tablespoons extra virgin olive oil

1 tablespoon coarse salt

for the sauce

2 tablespoons extra virgin olive oil

4 cloves garlic, peeled and left whole

1 28-ounce can whole peeled tomatoes with their juice

1 teaspoon coarse salt

for the toppings (choose a couple, or as many as you like)

Fresh mozzarella

Fresh basil leaves

Your best, highest-quality olive oil

Slowly cooked onions (For 2 pizzas, I like to cut 3 yellow onions into thin rounds and cook them on medium heat with a few spoonfuls of olive oil, a bay leaf, and a sprig of thyme until they're very soft and totally collapsed and caramelized, a good 25 minutes.)

Olive oil–packed Spanish anchovies

Olives

Parmesan cheese

Gorgonzola cheese

Truffle oil

If you have a wood fire, get it going a couple of hours before you want to eat pizza. If not, preheat a pizza stone in your oven at the highest heat it can go to for at least 1 hour before eating.

For the dough, whisk together ¾ cup of the water, the sugar, and the yeast in a large bowl and let stand until surface has a few little bubbles and is creamy, about 5 minutes. Add 1½ cups water, 3¾ cups of flour, olive oil, and salt, and stir until smooth. While stirring, gradually add up to another cup of flour until the dough starts to pull itself from the edges of the bowl.

Knead the dough on a generously floured surface until elastic and smooth—it will take about 8 minutes of hard work. Dust the surface with flour as you go—you don't want the dough to stick. Form the kneaded dough into a ball, dust with flour, and gently place in a large bowl and cover with plastic wrap. Let it rise in a warm spot until doubled, about 1½ hours. (You can let it sit for up to a couple of hours or even overnight in the refrigerator.)

For the sauce, meanwhile, heat the olive oil in a medium pot over medium heat with the garlic. Add the tomatoes and their juice and salt and bring to a boil. Lower the heat and let the sauce simmer for 1 hour. Cool it to room temperature and puree in the blender.

To assemble the pizzas, break off pieces of the dough and stretch them with your fingers until quite thin. Flour your pizza peel (the board you slide under the pizza) and place the dough on top (better to do this first as opposed to trying to transfer your fully loaded pizza onto the peel).

For the toppings, dress each pizza however you'd like. A slick of tomato sauce, a few torn pieces of mozzarella, and basil, and a drizzle of olive oil is classic for a reason. I like a heap of slowly cooked onions, a few anchovies, and some black olives. Four-cheese is also a winner, and, anointed with a little truffle oil, is a slice of heaven. However you choose, be sure to drizzle each pizza with good olive oil before sliding it into your hot oven. If you get them really thin and your oven is super hot, each pizza will cook in about 2 minutes. Most regular ovens will take more like 6 minutes. You're looking for a slightly charred crust and a top that is bubbling.

YIELD: 4–6 6-inch pizzas • ACTIVE PREPARATION TIME: 1 hour
TOTAL PREPARATION TIME: about 2½ hours

ten-hour chicken

THIS DISH IS GREAT when you are going to work in the morning but want a no-fuss meal when you get home. The long, slow cooking means the chicken basically braises in its own juices all day long. What you get is a falling-off-the-bone chicken, very tender and very juicy. Just make sure that the breast is down and you make a nice airtight seal with the foil. Then when you get home, remove the foil, turn the chicken over, and crisp up the skin, and you have one of the easiest working-parent dinners ever.

1 organic whole chicken (3-4 pounds), washed and dried (See Salt Scrubs for Poultry, page 43)

1 lemon, halved

Coarse salt

Freshly ground black pepper

½ bunch fresh thyme

Half a head of garlic, peeled

Preheat the oven to 200°F.

Place the chicken in a rectangular roasting dish breast side down. Squeeze the lemon halves over the chicken in the pan. Generously sprinkle the chicken with salt and pepper all over (front and back, inside and out). Tuck the thyme and the lemon halves and 3-4 cloves of garlic in the cavity. Place the remaining garlic cloves around the pan. Wrap the roasting dish tightly with aluminum foil and put it in the oven for, no joke, 9½ hours.

Take the chicken out of the oven and boost the heat to 400°F on convection if possible. Unwrap the dish, flip the chicken so it's lying on its back breast side up, and sprinkle with more salt and pepper. Roast for 15-20 minutes, or until it's nicely browned. Let the chicken cool slightly, then carve and serve with all of its lovely juices.

SERVES: 4 • ACTIVE PREPARATION TIME: 10 minutes • TOTAL PREPARATION TIME: about 10 hours
You put it up in the morning and don't worry about it until the evening.

broiled salmon with homemade teriyaki sauce

THIS DELICIOUS SALMON TERIYAKI RECIPE is the way that I got my son eating salmon (full of protein, omegas, etc., salmon has been hailed as a miracle food). The sauce has honey in it, so it gets crispy and sweet as it caramelizes. I like to make bigger fillets for the older set and bite-sized ones for the kids. It is really good.

¼ cup soy sauce

2 tablespoons mirin

3 tablespoons honey

⅓ cup water

1 teaspoon peeled and finely grated ginger

2 sprigs fresh cilantro

4 6-ounce salmon fillets, skin discarded

1 tablespoon finely minced fresh chives, for serving

Combine the soy sauce, mirin, honey, water, ginger, and cilantro in a small saucepan over high heat. Once it boils, turn the heat to low and let it simmer for 2 minutes. Remove the saucepan from the heat and let the sauce cool down. Once it's cool, pour into a large bowl or plastic bag and add the salmon. Marinate in the fridge for at least an hour, up to overnight.

When you're ready to eat, preheat the broiler.

Put the salmon on a heavy baking sheet with whatever sauce adheres to it and broil until cooked to your liking, 7–8 minutes. While it's cooking, strain the extra sauce into a clean saucepan, bring to a boil, and let it reduce.

To serve, drizzle the cooked salmon with some of the extra sauce and a sprinkle of chives.

make it kid friendly   Cut some of the salmon into 1-inch cubes, broil alongside the larger pieces, and serve without the chives—kids love these, especially if you call the teriyaki "honey sauce."

make it vegan   Replace the salmon with tofu.

SERVES: 4 · **ACTIVE PREPARATION TIME:** 20 minutes
TOTAL PREPARATION TIME: 1½ hours up to overnight

perfect roasted
chinese duck

THIS IS DEFINITELY FOR A PARTY meal or a big Sunday dinner. It takes some effort, but it's worth it. You must make the duck broth for the Duck Broth with Soba (page 52) the next day! Serve with Sesame Pancakes—or ready-made Chinese pancakes or flour tortillas—Red Miso Hoisin, cucumber matchsticks, and sliced scallions.

1   organic large duck, washed and dried (See Salt Scrubs for Poultry, page 43)

    Coarse salt

    Freshly ground black pepper

1   small yellow onion, peeled and quartered

2   star anise

⅛   teaspoon ground cloves

¼   cup dark brown sugar (unrefined if possible)

    Boiling water

1   cucumber, cut into matchsticks, for serving

1   bunch scallions, shredded, for serving

    Sesame Pancakes (page 180), for serving

    Red Miso Hoisin (page 180), for serving

Preheat the oven to 350°F.

Trim off excess skin from the opening to the cavity and from the back end of the duck (render it and save it for frying potatoes if you like). Use your fingers and the tip of a paring knife to slip underneath the skin covering the breast, loosening it and being careful not to tear it. Pierce the skin all over with the paring knife (approximately 50 times), but do not pierce the meat itself. This is to ensure that all the fat renders during cooking and you'll be rewarded with delicious, crispy skin.

Put the duck in a large roasting pan. Generously sprinkle salt and pepper over it, top to bottom, front and back. Stuff the cavity with the onion and star anise. Put the duck breast side up in the pan and sprinkle with ground cloves. Sprinkle the brown sugar all around the duck, not on it. Pour enough boiling water over the duck and into the pan to come up 1 inch (to tighten the skin).

Cover the pan very tightly with aluminum foil. Bake for 1 hour, flip it, cover it again with the foil, and bake for an additional hour. Transfer the duck to a plate and let it cool.

Meanwhile, put the roasting pan on your stovetop and boil the liquid over high heat for 20-30 minutes, or until reduced by about half. Cool slightly and pour it into a storage container. Wrap up both the duck and the liquid and refrigerate overnight.

To finish the duck, preheat the oven to 500°F.

Roast the duck for 25 minutes, or until crispy and browned. Let it rest for at least 10 minutes before serving.

To serve, use your reserved pan juices. A significant amount of fat should be hardened on the top—scoop it off and discard. Put the dark brown juice in a small saucepan and warm it over medium heat. Carve the duck into thin slices. Pour the warm juice over the slices. Wrap up bits of duck, cucumbers, and scallions in Sesame Pancakes spread with Red Miso Hoisin sauce.

SERVES: 4 • ACTIVE PREPARATION TIME: 20 minutes
TOTAL PREPARATION TIME: 2½ hours plus overnight refrigeration

sesame pancakes

1 cup unbleached all-purpose flour

1½ cups rice milk

Pinch salt

2 teaspoons toasted sesame oil

1 teaspoon vegetable oil

Whisk together the flour, milk, salt, and sesame oil. Heat a small nonstick skillet (I use a 6-inch skillet) over medium heat. Pour in the vegetable oil and use a paper towel to spread it evenly. Pour in 2 tablespoons of batter and swirl the skillet to coat the bottom. Cook for about 30 seconds, or until browned on the bottom. Peel the pancake up from the skillet and flip it (it's fastest to loosen the edges with a butter knife or rubber spatula and then lift it up with your fingers). Cook for about 30 seconds on the second side. The first one's usually a dud. That's okay. Continue the process until you run out of batter. You should end up with about a dozen pancakes.

note: You can make these ahead and then quickly heat them up for a few seconds on each side in a hot, nonstick pan—much easier than trying to make them all last minute!

 YIELD: about 1 dozen pancakes • ACTIVE & TOTAL PREPARATION TIME: 20 minutes

red miso hoisin

THIS IS SO MUCH HEALTHIER than a commercial version!

1 tablespoon grapeseed or vegetable oil

1 large clove garlic, peeled and minced

½ teaspoon Chinese five-spice powder

½ cup red miso

½ cup real Vermont maple syrup

2 tablespoons brown rice vinegar

Heat the grapeseed oil in a small saucepan over medium heat. Add the garlic and five-spice powder and cook for about 30 seconds, or until wonderfully fragrant. Whisk in the remaining ingredients, bring to a boil, and cook, whisking or stirring constantly, for 3-4 minutes, or until slightly thickened. Let the sauce cool before using. It keeps well in the refrigerator for a few days.

YIELD: about 1 cup • ACTIVE & TOTAL PREPARATION TIME: about 5 minutes

crab boil

SO MY DECEASED MATERNAL GRANDMOTHER, Mutti, was a great entertainer (but not actually that nice one on one, at least to me!). She was amazing at a party and she used to throw them all the time. She was famous for them. One of her old-school recipes was this crab boil for a dinner party. Her original method for making the crab is just as I have it here. It works beautifully. I modified the sauce a bit as the original used a lot of premade sauces with too many preservatives.

1 fresh bay leaf

5 black peppercorns

2 cloves

Pinch coarse salt

1 large clove garlic, peeled and crushed

1 lemon, halved

2 large live crabs

Sauce for Crab Boil (recipe follows)

Fill your largest pot with water, add the bay leaf, peppercorns, cloves, salt, and garlic, and squeeze in the juice from the lemon (throw the lemon halves into the pot too). Bring the seasoned water to a boil and let it boil for 10–15 minutes. Add the crabs and boil for 15 minutes. Remove them to a tray and let them sit until cool enough to handle. Get to work with a mallet and a pick, getting all the bits of meat out of the claws and body. You can do this for your guests and serve everyone a pile of pristine crabmeat with a bowl of sauce alongside or you can all stand in the kitchen and do it together, dipping bits of crab as you work.

SERVES: 4 • ACTIVE PREPARATION TIME: 20 minutes • TOTAL PREPARATION TIME: 1 hour

You can serve it cold.

sauce for crab boil

½ cup Vegenaise

1 tablespoon plus 1 teaspoon ketchup

2 teaspoons Dijon mustard

2 teaspoons prepared horseradish

2 teaspoons finely chopped fresh chives

4 cornichons, finely diced

Coarse salt

Freshly ground black pepper

Stir everything together, seasoning to taste with salt and pepper.

YIELD: ¾ cup • ACTIVE & TOTAL PREPARATION TIME: 10 minutes

duck "cassoulet"

I FIRST HAD DUCK CONFIT with my dad on a trip to Paris at a place called Josephine Chez Dumonet. I never realized how delicious, tender, and yet crispy duck could be. When I discovered cassoulet (in which duck confit is the star) I was transported. When I stopped eating pork and red meat, I couldn't indulge in it anymore, so I set out to make my own. This pork-free version is rich and deeply flavored—a great one-pot weekend supper. I wish I could make it for my dad, he would go out of his mind.

2 14-ounce cans cannellini beans, rinsed and drained

1 big dark green leaf from the outside of a leek

7 cloves peeled garlic, 3 crushed, 4 finely sliced

Coarse salt

Bouquet garni of 3 sprigs fresh parsley, 1 sprig chervil, 2 cloves, 1 bay leaf, and 6 peppercorns

4 slices duck bacon, fat removed from all but 1, chopped into lardoons

1 medium yellow onion, peeled and finely chopped

1 14-ounce can whole peeled tomatoes with their juice

Freshly ground black pepper

4 legs duck confit, excess fat scraped off (strain the fat and save it for cooking delicious potatoes!)

2 tablespoons extra virgin olive oil

½ day-old baguette, cut into coarse crumbs (or pulsed 10 times in a food processor)

1 tablespoon chopped fresh parsley

2 sprigs fresh thyme

Combine the beans, leek leaf, 1 crushed clove garlic, a large pinch of salt, and the bouquet garni in a large saucepan. Cover with cold water, bring to a boil, and lower the heat. Let it simmer over low heat while you proceed.

In a large heavy pot, cook the duck bacon over medium-high heat for 3 minutes, or until beginning to render and brown. Turn the heat to low and add the onion and the 4 sliced cloves garlic. Cook for 15 minutes, keeping the heat low. Add the tomatoes and their juice, crushing them with a wooden spoon, a pinch of salt, and a few healthy grinds of black pepper. Simmer on low for half an hour.

Meanwhile, put the duck legs in a large frying pan and set it over medium heat. Let the duck legs brown deeply on both sides, about 5 minutes a side, and remove to a plate, reserving the fat in the pan. Add the olive oil to the pan along with the 2 remaining crushed cloves garlic, keeping the heat at medium. Add the bread crumbs and cook, stirring, until fragrant, about 2 minutes. Remove from heat, discard the garlic, and stir in the parsley.

At this point your tomato mixture should be cooked down. Drain the beans, reserving their cooking liquid and discarding the leek, garlic, and bouquet garni. Stir the beans into the tomato mixture, nestle in the thyme and the duck legs. Season with salt and pepper.

At this point, you can wait up to a day or two to cook the cassoulet—refrigerate the bean and duck mixture, bean liquid, and bread crumbs separately and bring to room temperature before proceeding. Or, preheat the oven to 350°F. To finish, scatter the bread crumbs over the top of the cassoulet and evenly ladle over 1½ cups of the bean cooking liquid. Bake in the 350°F oven until the bread crumbs are nicely browned, about ½ hour.

SERVES: 4 • ACTIVE PREPARATION TIME: 1 hour • TOTAL PREPARATION TIME: 1½ hours

grilled "baked stuffed" lobsters

BAKED, STUFFED LOBSTER HAS ALWAYS been one of my absolute favorite East Coast special-occasion dinners. This version gets a smoky, charred flavor from the grill, but is equally delish done under the broiler. The trick of the stuffing is to chop up the roe and tomalley and mix them in with the other ingredients—also the Vegenaise adds a delicious moistness.

2	1½-pound lobsters
1¼	cups, fresh coarse bread crumbs (pulse day-old bread in the food processor)
2½	tablespoons dried bread crumbs
5	tablespoons unsalted butter, melted and divided
3	ounces jumbo lump crabmeat, shredded with your fingers
⅓	cup rock shrimp, chopped, or extra crabmeat
1	tablespoon finely chopped fresh parsley
½	teaspoon coarse salt
¼	teaspoon freshly ground black pepper
2	teaspoons fresh lemon juice
3	tablespoons Vegenaise, divided

Preheat the grill over high heat.

Cut the lobsters in half: first insert a sharp knife swiftly through their eyes and then cut straight down through their tails. Scoop out any roe and finely chop it. In a large bowl, mix the roe with both the fresh and dried bread crumbs, 2 tablespoons of the butter, the crab, shrimp, parsley, salt, pepper, lemon juice, and 2 tablespoons of the Vegenaise. In a separate small bowl, whisk together the remaining tablespoon of Vegenaise with the remaining 3 tablespoons of butter. Evenly divide the stuffing along the cut sides of the lobsters and evenly drizzle over the Vegenaise-butter mixture. Carefully lay the lobsters on a large sheet pan and put the pan directly on the hot grill. Cover and cook for 15 minutes, or until the stuffing is browned (the grill acts as an oven) and the lobster meat is just firm to the touch.

notes: You can make these indoors—simply roast them at 450°F for about 15 minutes to cook everything through and then broil them for 2 minutes to brown the tops.

As an alternative to lobster, you can stuff the filling into butterflied jumbo shrimp that you've seasoned with salt and pepper (these take only 10 minutes to cook). Delish.

SERVES: 4 · ACTIVE PREPARATION TIME: 10 minutes · TOTAL PREPARATION TIME: ½ hour

You can stuff the lobsters ahead of time.

aunt evelyn's brisket (by way of grandma vicki & grandma dorothy)

MY FATHER'S BROTHER, BOBBY, married a girl named Evelyn a long, long time ago. Evelyn is a Sephardic Jew and had an amazing mother, the matriarch of the family, Grandma Vicki. My paternal grandmother, Dorothy, lived down the street from Grandma Vicki, and they would frequently break bread together. They all made brisket, and each family was famous for its own version. Although I have not eaten red meat for years, I remember the days of eating this brisket and loving the tender, falling-apart meat, which was always served with butter noodles. When I was working on the recipes for this family book, I felt I had to include a brisket to be true to the long line of Paltrow, Weigert, and Hertz women before me for whom this dish was so essential. We got all of the recipes together (one included dry-rubbing the meat with Lipton onion soup mix!) and devised a way to amalgamate and elevate all at the same time. Julia Turshen, my right hand in helping me put this book together, did the tasting with her mother and grandmother, and it got a big thumbs-up.

1   3-pound brisket

1   tablespoon paprika

2   cloves garlic, peeled and finely minced

1   teaspoon coarse salt

½   teaspoon freshly ground black pepper

7   tablespoons extra virgin olive oil, divided

2   large yellow onions, peeled and thinly sliced

4   carrots, peeled and cut into 3-inch pieces

2   cups good red wine

½   cup Chicken Stock (page 39)

Preheat the oven to 300°F.

Trim the brisket of any excess fat. Meanwhile, stir together the paprika, garlic, salt, pepper, and 1 tablespoon of the olive oil. Rub this spice mixture all over the brisket and let it sit at room temperature while you cook the vegetables.

Heat 2 tablespoons of the olive oil in a large sauté pan over medium-high heat. Cook the onions, stirring occasionally, until softened and lightly browned, about 10 minutes. Place the onions in the bottom of a 9 x 13-inch casserole dish and return the pan to the heat with 2 additional tablespoons of olive oil. Add the carrots to the pan and cook, stirring occasionally, until lightly browned, about 5 minutes. Add the carrots to the onions. Return the pan to the stove, turn the heat to high, and add 2 more tablespoons of olive oil. Deeply brown the brisket on both sides, about 4 minutes a side. Place the brisket on top of the vegetables. Add the wine to the pan, bring to a boil, and let it cook for 3 minutes. Pour the wine and the chicken stock over the brisket and vegetables.

Cover the casserole tightly with foil and bake for 3 hours. Remove the brisket from the casserole and let it cool while you finish the sauce. Blend half of the cooked vegetables with about 1 cup of the cooking liquid in a blender until smooth. Return the blended mixture to the remaining vegetables and juice (this helps to thicken the sauce). Slice the brisket as thinly as you like it and either serve immediately or place the slices in the sauce, wrap tightly, and reheat in a 300°F oven when ready to serve.

SERVES: 4, with leftovers • ACTIVE PREPARATION TIME: 20 minutes • TOTAL PREPARATION TIME: 3–4 hours

side
dishes

A couple of great-looking little dishes can be so comforting and sometimes unexpected, all while celebrating or reinventing the vegetable it features. While rounding out a main dish with a perfect side really elevates the whole meal, sometimes my entire dinner will consist of lots of little veggie dishes, especially great for punching up the vegetarian excitement factor. In the summer when my favorite vegetarian friend, Stella McCartney, brings her family over, I like to double the recipes and make a vegetarian buffet, sometimes Italian (bruschetta, burrata with roasted beets, roasted peppers, stuffed artichokes, zucchini flowers) or East Coast summer (garlic bread from GOOP.com, corn fritters, and a simple bean salad).

sautéed greens with onions & soy sauce

THIS HEALTHY SIDE DISH has tons of flavor from the sharp greens, sweet onions, and soy sauce. Winter greens have many nutrients, so I love for my family to partake of them.

2 tablespoons extra virgin olive oil

1 small yellow onion, peeled and thinly sliced

1 pound seasonal greens (kale, Swiss chard, dandelion, etc.), stems removed and discarded, leaves washed and roughly torn

½ cup water

1½ tablespoons soy sauce

Heat the olive oil in a large skillet over medium-high heat. Cook the onion, stirring occasionally for 5–7 minutes, or until just softened and a little crisp on the edges. Add about half the greens and the water—these will wilt significantly after a minute or two. Add the remaining greens and stir for another 3 minutes, or until the greens are wilted but still maintain a little bite. Add the soy sauce, cook for one more minute, and serve.

 SERVES: 4 generously · ACTIVE & TOTAL PREPARATION TIME: 10 minutes

roasted cauliflower

ROASTING CAULIFLOWER SLOWLY IN OLIVE OIL brings out incredible sweetness and crunch—two things that go over big with the little ones. My kids love these. They are great as a side or chopped into a vegetable salad.

1 head cauliflower, hard core discarded, cut into small florets

2 tablespoons extra virgin olive oil

Pinch coarse salt

Pinch freshly ground black pepper

Preheat the oven to 450°F.

In a baking dish large enough to hold the cauliflower in one layer, toss all the ingredients together. Roast for 35 minutes, stirring occasionally, until the cauliflower is caramelized all over. So simple and so unbelievably good.

SERVES: 4 · **ACTIVE PREPARATION TIME:** 5 minutes
TOTAL PREPARATION TIME: 40 minutes

crispy potato & garlic cake

I FIRST ATE SOMETHING AKIN to this dish at Chez L'Ami Louis in Paris, my father's favorite restaurant maybe in the world. They serve a sizzling hot, garlicky version of this pie—which I started re-creating in my own kitchen a few years ago. I'm not sure how they do theirs, but this is definitely an homage to their masterpiece. I love it served with a roast or duck confit, French style.

2 large baking potatoes (each about ²⁄₃ pound), peeled

¼ cup plus 1 tablespoon duck fat (the tablespoon is for the pan, or you can use butter)

¼ cup extra virgin olive oil

3 cloves peeled garlic, 2 crushed, 1 very finely minced

Coarse salt

1 tablespoon finely chopped fresh parsley

Preheat the broiler.

Boil the potatoes for 20 minutes and let them cool before slicing them into ⅛-inch-thick slices. Heat a spoonful each of the duck fat and the olive oil in a large nonstick frying pan over medium heat. Add 1 of the crushed garlic cloves and as many potato slices as can fit in one layer. Cook for about 3 minutes a side, or until lightly browned. Remove to a paper towel–lined plate and repeat with the remaining fat and potatoes, switching out the garlic cloves when they get too brown.

Coat a small (6–8-inch) cast-iron skillet with the tablespoon of duck fat. Line the bottom with a single layer of potato slices, sprinkle with salt, and add another layer. Repeat this process, pressing each layer down hard with the back of a wooden spoon and lightly salting as you go until you've layered all your potatoes. Pressing them down is what will keep the cake together, so don't be too gentle. Stick the cake under the broiler until really browned and crispy, about 5 minutes. Invert it onto a plate and scatter with the 1 clove of finely minced garlic, parsley, and bit more salt if you like. Cut into wedges and serve.

SERVES: 4 · ACTIVE & TOTAL PREPARATION TIME: a little under 1 hour

This can be made ahead up until the point of broiling.

maple-dijon roasted winter vegetables

KIDS AND ADULTS ALIKE DEVOUR these sweet roasted vegetables. Any hearty root vegetables will work—butternut squash, turnips, etc. Whatever the combo, the maple syrup and mustard marry the flavors and turn them into a crowd pleaser.

3 tablespoons real Vermont maple syrup

3 tablespoons Dijon mustard

3 tablespoons extra virgin olive oil

½ teaspoon coarse salt

½ teaspoon freshly ground black pepper

1 large sweet potato, peeled and cut into 3-inch sticks about ½-inch thick (like French fries)

4 parsnips, peeled and cut into 3-inch sticks about ½-inch thick (like French fries)

4 carrots, peeled and cut into 3-inch sticks about ½-inch thick (like French fries)

Preheat the oven to 425°F.

Mix together the maple syrup, mustard, olive oil, salt, and pepper. Toss together with the vegetables on a cookie sheet. Roast, stirring occasionally, until browned and cooked through, about 25 minutes.

SERVES: 4 • ACTIVE PREPARATION TIME: 10 minutes
TOTAL PREPARATION TIME: about ½ hour

caramelized brussels sprouts

I HAVE CONVERTED MANY a sprout cynic with these crispy, crunchy Brussels sprouts. I must make these three times a week when they are in season. They go with anything and are the opposite of your grandmother's overboiled cabbage-tasting variety.

1 pound Brussels sprouts, trimmed

2 tablespoons extra virgin olive oil

A few generous pinches coarse salt

Your best, highest-quality olive oil, for serving

½ lemon, for serving

Steam the Brussels sprouts for 7 minutes, or until just tender. Let them cool a bit and then cut each in half lengthwise.

Heat the olive oil in a large skillet over medium-high heat. Place the Brussels sprouts in a single layer cut side down (in batches if necessary). Leave them for 4–5 minutes, allowing them to brown thoroughly and evenly—don't give in to the temptation to stir and toss them! Keep an eye on them though—the key is to have the flame high enough to brown them but low enough not to burn them. When they've browned, flip each one and let the other side get color, an additional 3 minutes or so. Remove to a serving platter, sprinkle with the salt, drizzle with your best olive oil, and squeeze the lemon over the Brussel sprouts, trying to get a bit of juice on each one. Delish.

SERVES: 4 • **ACTIVE & TOTAL PREPARATION TIME:** 20 minutes

fried rice with kale & scallions

MY KIDS CALL THIS GREEN RICE and they love it. Oh how my heart leaps when I see them munching down kale with brown rice. The smaller you cut the kale, the more it becomes about the rice. I love it when something this nutritious tastes so good.

½ pound kale, stems discarded

1½ tablespoons vegetable oil

2 cloves garlic, peeled and very finely minced

3 large scallions, cut into ⅛-inch diagonal slices

2½ cups cooked brown rice

1 tablespoon plus 1 teaspoon soy sauce

Cut the kale leaves in half lengthwise and then cut crosswise into very thin ribbons (chiffonade). Steam the kale for 7 minutes.

Meanwhile, heat the vegetable oil in a large saucepan over medium-low heat. Add the garlic and cook, stirring, for 2 minutes, being careful not to brown the garlic. Raise the heat to medium and add the steamed kale and scallions. Cook for 2 minutes and then add the rice and cook for another 2 minutes, stirring. Add the soy sauce and cook for 30 seconds more.

SERVES: 4 · ACTIVE & TOTAL PREPARATION TIME: 15 minutes

roasted sweet potatoes with spices

SWEET POTATOES ARE A BIG family fave. These accentuate the innate sweetness with some maple syrup—making them soft and caramelized. The spices make them nice for the holidays as well.

1¼ pounds sweet potatoes (about 2 medium), peeled

⅓ cup real Vermont maple syrup

2 tablespoons vegetable oil

¼ teaspoon ground cinnamon

⅛ teaspoon ground cloves

1 large orange

1 star anise

Preheat the oven to 375°F.

Cut each sweet potato in half horizontally and then cut each half into ⅓-inch-thick slices (about 4 slices per half depending on the size of the sweet potato). Lay the sweet potatoes in a single layer in a large earthenware baking dish that's been lined with a piece of parchment (makes cleanup much easier).

Mix the maple syrup, vegetable oil, cinnamon, and cloves together in a small bowl. Peel off 2 large strips of zest from the orange. Cut the orange in half and squeeze the juice from one half into the bowl with the maple syrup mixture. Pour this mixture evenly over the sweet potatoes, nestle in the strips of zest, and the star anise. Bake for 45 minutes, or until the sweet potatoes are soft.

SERVES: 4 • **ACTIVE PREPARATION TIME: 10 minutes**
TOTAL PREPARATION TIME: a little less than 1 hour

kale chips

THESE THINGS ARE A SUREFIRE WAY to get your family eating this
nutrient-rich vegetable. They crisp up in the oven and sort of mimic potato
chips. My kids eat them like they actually are potato chips: they don't stop.

1 big bunch kale, stems
  discarded and leaves
  torn into roughly 1½-inch
  pieces

2 tablespoons extra virgin
  olive oil

  Coarse salt

Preheat the oven to 400°F.

Toss the kale with the olive oil and spread out on two baking sheets.
Sprinkle with coarse salt and roast for 12–15 minutes, or until lightly browned
and crispy. Eat like potato chips.

SERVES: 4 • ACTIVE PREPARATION TIME: 2 minutes • TOTAL PREPARATION TIME: 15 minutes

deli coleslaw

I HAVE YET TO FIND deli coleslaw that's the real deal in England (where I
live during the school year). This one really hits the spot when I'm dreaming
of a New York deli lunch or a BBQ. It's got that authentic taste. I put it directly
on my sandwiches.

½ small green cabbage,
  coarsely grated (about
  2 cups)

  Coarse salt

½ carrot, peeled and coarsely
  grated

½ cup Vegenaise

2 teaspoons apple cider
  vinegar

2 teaspoons granulated
  sugar

Toss the cabbage with a healthy pinch of salt and let sit for at least
10 minutes. Add the rest of the ingredients and stir to combine. Let the
coleslaw get to know itself for at least an hour or 2, but this is really best
when you let it sit overnight.

SERVES: 4 • ACTIVE PREPARATION TIME: 15 minutes
TOTAL PREPARATION TIME: 15 minutes plus at least 1 hour resting

french fries: two ways

HERE WE HAVE TWO VERSIONS of one of my favorite foods on earth: the French fry. The "no-fry" version produces a crispy, delicious fry when you don't want the deep-fry effect on your health. The fried version is, well, fried, and therefore even more delicious.

NO-FRY FRIES

2 large russet potatoes (each about ²/₃ pound), peeled

2 tablespoons olive oil

¾ teaspoon coarse salt

Preheat the oven to 450°F.

Cut each potato in half horizontally and then cut each half into long, ⅓-inch-thick sticks. Put the potatoes in a bowl of cold water as you're cutting them. Dry them completely on paper towels (dry potatoes = crispy French fries). Coat the potatoes with the olive oil and sprinkle with the salt. Roast on a cooling rack set on top of a cookie sheet until browned and cooked through, turning a few times as you go, about 25 minutes.

 SERVES: 4 · **ACTIVE PREPARATION TIME:** 10 minutes · **TOTAL PREPARATION TIME:** ½ hour

REAL FRENCH FRIES

2 large dense floury (not waxy) baking potatoes (each about ²/₃ pound), peeled

Safflower oil for frying

Coarse salt

Cut each potato in half horizontally and then cut each half into long, ⅓-inch-thick sticks. Put the potatoes in a bowl of cold water as you're cutting them and let them soak for at least ½ hour and up to overnight. Dry them completely on clean tea towels, really paying attention to each side (painstaking, yes, but worth it, as dry potatoes = crispy French fries). In a deep-fat fryer or large heavy pot, heat enough safflower oil for deep frying (the oil should be at least 4 inches deep) to 300°F. Fry the potatoes in batches for 4–5 minutes, stirring a bit with a slotted spoon, until light golden brown. Drain the potatoes on a cookie rack set on top of a sheet pan and let them cool as you continue with the remaining potatoes. Once all the potatoes have been through the first fry, raise the heat to 375°F and fry them again in batches for about 2 more minutes or until darker brown and crisp. Drain them on a rack, sprinkle liberally with salt, and serve immediately.

 SERVES: 4 · **ACTIVE PREPARATION TIME:** 30 minutes · **TOTAL PREPARATION TIME:** 1 hour

polenta with fresh corn

POLENTA IS A WONDERFUL CREAMY GRAIN, very healthy, and a neutral flavor—making it a canvas to showcase your favorite ingredients like cheeses, truffles, veggies, and the like. During the summer when sweet corn is rife, I like to stir it into polenta for a double hit of corn—a corn celebration. You can cut the leftovers into squares and fry them topped with Parmesan.

4	cups water
1	cup polenta
	Coarse salt
	Kernels from 1 fresh ear of corn
½	cup milk
¼	cup cream
	Freshly ground black pepper
1	tablespoon roughly chopped fresh chives, for serving

Bring the water to a boil in a small soup pot. Slowly whisk in the polenta and a pinch of salt. Turn the heat as low as it can go, put a lid on slightly ajar, and cook the polenta for 40 minutes, stirring every 5–10 minutes. Add the corn, milk, and cream and cook for 5 minutes. Season with salt and pepper and serve sprinkled with chives.

SERVES: 4 • ACTIVE PREPARATION TIME: 20 minutes • TOTAL PREPARATION TIME: 50 minutes

stuffed artichokes
with bread & tomatoes

I WANTED TO RE-CREATE one of my favorite side dishes I enjoyed at DaSilvano's, stuffed artichokes. After a few tries, I came up with this recipe. It takes a typical northern Italian pairing—day-old bread and tomatoes—and puts it in a steamed artichoke. It's a lovely side, especially with extra vinaigrette in which to dip the artichoke leaves—or it can serve as a light lunch.

4   artichokes, top inch and tough outer leaves cut off and discarded

½   cup plus 2 tablespoons extra virgin olive oil

3   tablespoons red wine vinegar

    Coarse salt

    Freshly ground black pepper

4   cups day-old ½-inch bread cubes (about ½ stale baguette will do)

2   cups cherry tomatoes, quartered

    Handful fresh basil leaves, torn

1   lemon

Steam the artichokes for 45 minutes.

Meanwhile, whisk together the ½ cup of olive oil and vinegar and season with salt and pepper. Fold in the bread cubes. If they're really dry, add a spoonful of warm water. Using your hands, crush in the tomatoes and stir in the basil. Let the bread mixture sit while the artichokes are cooking.

When the artichokes are cooked through, let them sit for 10 or 15 minutes to cool. Using a soup spoon, scoop out the thistly chokes. Squeeze the lemon over the cavity of each artichoke and stuff with the bread salad. Drizzle over the remaining 2 tablespoons of olive oil. Serve at room temperature.

SERVES: 4 • ACTIVE PREPARATION TIME: 10 minutes • TOTAL PREPARATION TIME: 1 hour

bruce's dip

MY DAD USED TO WHIP UP this dip and serve it in half of a ripe avocado—it was a summertime staple with a sandwich on the side.

1 cup Vegenaise

½ cup sour cream

2 tablespoons finely chopped fresh parsley

½ teaspoon Dijon mustard

2 scallions, finely sliced

1 clove garlic, peeled and minced or pushed through a press

½ teaspoon fresh lemon juice

A few fresh grinds black pepper

Pinch coarse salt

1½ tablespoons capers, finely chopped

¼ teaspoon celery seeds

Mix it all up.

SERVES: 4 • ACTIVE & TOTAL PREPARATION TIME: 5 minutes

corn fritters

MY GREAT FRIEND ROB (the husband of my oldest and best friend, Mary) made a version of these a few summers ago. I loved them so much I decided to try my own. These are wonderful when the summer corn is sweet and abundant—I like them as a side dish or served on a bed of arugula as a main course for lunch.

4 fresh ears of corn, shucked

1 organic large egg, beaten

⅓ cup packed grated Parmesan cheese

¼ cup packed grated sharp Cheddar cheese

2 scallions (white and light green parts), finely sliced

¼ cup unbleached all-purpose flour

1½ teaspoons cornstarch

¼ teaspoon freshly ground black pepper

¼ teaspoon coarse salt, plus more for finishing

¼ cup vegetable oil

10 fresh large basil leaves

2 tablespoons fresh cilantro leaves

Cut the corn kernels off of the cobs and discard the cobs. Combine the corn, egg, cheeses, scallions, flour, cornstarch, pepper, and ¼ teaspoon of salt together in a large mixing bowl. Heat the vegetable oil in a medium nonstick skillet over medium-high heat. Pour the fritter batter onto the skillet using a ¼-cup measure and fry for 2 minutes on each side, or until dark golden brown and very attractive. Drain the fritters on paper towels, sprinkle with salt, and keep warm while you repeat the process with the remaining batter. Roughly chop the basil and cilantro leaves and scatter on top of the fritters.

YIELD: *8 fritters* • ACTIVE & TOTAL PREPARATION TIME: *20 minutes*

zucchini flowers with anchovies & mozzarella

WHEN I PASS A FLOWERING ZUCCHINI plant in a garden, my heart skips a beat. They are so delicious stuffed and fried, it's crazy. I have friends who make them with meat in the center but my favorite is this version—with anchovies and mozzarella. You can substitute a squeeze of lemon with its zest for anchovies to make a vegetarian version.

¾ cup unbleached all-purpose flour

1½ tablespoons extra virgin olive oil

¾ cup sparkling water or seltzer

Coarse salt

6 ounces fresh mozzarella (water packed), coarsely grated

6 anchovy fillets, finely chopped

¼ teaspoon freshly ground black pepper

20 small zucchini flowers

Safflower or peanut oil, for frying

1 lemon, halved, for serving

Whisk the flour together with the olive oil in a large bowl—the mixture will be pebbly. Whisk the fizzy water into the mixture until the batter is smooth. Season with a large pinch of salt, cover with plastic, and let sit for at least 30 minutes.

Meanwhile, mix together the mozzarella, anchovies, pepper, and a pinch of salt in a mixing bowl with a wooden spoon. Carefully open each zucchini flower and stuff it with a generous tablespoon of filling, twisting the top ever so gently just to keep everything inside—you want to try not to tear the flowers, but a break or two is inevitable, so don't drive yourself crazy. At this point, the batter and the flowers can be set aside for up to a couple of hours.

When you're ready to eat, heat up an inch of oil in a large cast-iron skillet or other heavy pan with a bit of height over medium-high heat. When a drop of water or small cube of bread sizzles on contact, dip each zucchini flower into the batter just to coat it and carefully slip it into the oil. Fill the pan with as many flowers as will fit in a single layer without overcrowding. Brown the flowers on both sides (about 45 seconds a side) and then drain on paper towels. Serve hot, squeezing a bit of lemon juice and sprinkling salt over each.

SERVES: 4 • ACTIVE & TOTAL PREPARATION TIME: 45 minutes

You can make this ahead up until the point of frying.

bruschetta (or "garlic toast" as my daughter calls it)

THIS IS ONE OF MY most asked-for sides, and probably the easiest. A slightly charred, garlic-and-oil-rubbed bread that makes any meal sing. The better and fresher the bread, the better the bruschetta, so it's definitely worth visiting the bakery for a rustic loaf such as pane Pugliese to maximize the perfection.

1 loaf pane Pugliese (or your favorite country-style bread), cut into ¾-inch-thick slices

2 large cloves garlic, peeled and cut in half

Extra virgin olive oil

Coarse salt

Grill the bread over a medium flame for about a minute on each side, or until toasted and just barely charred at spots. Rub both sides of bread with the cut sides of garlic. Drizzle one side generously with olive oil (at least 1½ tablespoons per slice). Sprinkle with coarse salt and serve.

SERVES: 4 · ACTIVE & TOTAL PREPARATION TIME: 10 minutes

fragrant jasmine rice

JASMINE RICE IS A LIFESAVER—it cooks so quickly, it's perfect for a last-minute grain. This version uses star anise and cardamom to accent the fine grain with some Asian flavor.

1 cup jasmine rice (or substitute brown jasmine rice for a healthy alternative and follow timing directions)

1¾ cups water

1 whole star anise

2 whole cardamom pods, seeds separated and pods discarded

Big pinch Maldon salt

Combine everything in a small pot, bring to a boil, lower to a simmer, cover, and cook for 15 minutes. Turn off the heat and let the rice sit for 10 minutes with the cover on. Fluff with a fork and serve.

note: Follow the rice-to-water ratio on whatever brand of rice you use.

SERVES: 4 • **ACTIVE PREPARATION TIME:** 5 minutes
TOTAL PREPARATION TIME: 25 minutes

breakfast

They say that breakfast is the most important meal of the day…I have some real breakfast fanatics in my house who would agree with that sentiment. With barely any extra effort, breakfast is an opportunity to speak to your loved ones' individualism. Pancakes plain? With chocolate chips and bananas? Thinned out to make a crepe with Nutella or Gruyère? Everyone can express their tastes, quirky or not. Bagel toasted with nova and cream cheese? Buttered? Untoasted onion bagel with peanut butter and jam?—not okay by the way. Food preferences are easy to contend with—set out a large bowl of granola and have all different fixin's on the side—berries, flax meal, yogurt, cow's milk, soy milk, hemp milk. Choices abound with only minor adjustments for the cook…making everyone feel loved with their breakfast served just the way they like it.

artichoke & parmesan frittata

I MAKE FRITTATAS FREQUENTLY when people come over for brunch. They are easy and delicious and you can use whatever is in the fridge—or in season. You really can follow the technique below and dream up anything you like. They can be served anywhere from hot to room temperature, a plus for reducing stress when serving multiple dishes at brunch.

1 tablespoon unsalted butter

1 tablespoon extra virgin olive oil

2 large shallots, peeled and thinly sliced

1 cup cooked artichoke hearts, cut into ¼-inch-thick slices

1 teaspoon fresh tarragon leaves, thinly sliced

Coarse salt

Freshly ground black pepper

6 organic large eggs

½ cup milk

2 ounces Parmesan cheese, grated (about ⅓ cup)

Preheat the oven to 375°F.

Heat the butter and olive oil over medium heat in a 10-inch cast-iron skillet. Sauté the shallots until soft and just barely browned, about 6 minutes. Add the artichokes and tarragon and season with salt and pepper to taste.

Meanwhile, beat the eggs and milk to combine in a mixing bowl. Pour over the shallots and artichokes. Let it cook for about 5 minutes, or until just set on the edges (it will still be very runny in the middle). Sprinkle the top with cheese and stick it in the oven for exactly 8 minutes; it should be just set throughout.

 SERVES: 4 • **ACTIVE PREPARATION TIME:** 20 minutes • **TOTAL PREPARATION TIME:** ½ hour

slow-roasted tomato, basil & smoked mozzarella frittata

1 tablespoon unsalted butter

1 tablespoon extra virgin olive oil

2 large shallots, peeled and thinly sliced

Coarse salt

Freshly ground black pepper

6 organic large eggs

½ cup soy milk

6 halves (3 whole) Slow-Roasted Tomatoes (page 32), each cut in half

1 small bowl (about 6 ounces) lightly smoked mozzarella, torn into bite-sized pieces

2 fresh large basil leaves, roughly torn

Preheat the oven to 375°F.

Heat the butter and olive oil over medium heat in a 10-inch cast-iron skillet. Sauté the shallots until soft and just barely browned, about 6 minutes. Season with plenty of salt and ground pepper.

Meanwhile, beat the eggs and soy milk in a mixing bowl. Pour over the shallots. Evenly distribute the tomatoes, cheese, and basil. Let it cook for about 5 minutes, or until just set on the edges (it will still be very runny in the middle). Stick it in the oven for exactly 8 minutes; it should be just set throughout.

SERVES: 4 • ACTIVE PREPARATION TIME: 20 minutes • TOTAL PREPARATION TIME: ½ hour

leek & gruyère frittata

- 1 tablespoon unsalted butter
- 1 tablespoon extra virgin olive oil
- 1 large leek, washed and very thinly sliced
- Coarse salt
- Freshly ground black pepper
- 6 organic large eggs
- ½ cup milk
- 2 ounces Gruyère cheese, grated (about ⅓ cup)

Preheat the oven to 375°F.

Heat the butter and olive oil over medium heat in a 10-inch cast-iron skillet. Sauté the leek slices until soft and just barely browned, 6–8 minutes. Season with plenty of salt and pepper.

Meanwhile, beat the eggs and milk to combine in a mixing bowl. Pour over the leek slices. Sprinkle the top with the cheese. Let it cook for about 5 minutes, or until just set on the edges (it will still be very runny in the middle). Stick it in the oven for exactly 8 minutes; it should be just set throughout.

SERVES: 4 • ACTIVE PREPARATION TIME: 20 minutes • TOTAL PREPARATION TIME: ½ hour

morning pancakes

I ADD YOGURT TO THESE PANCAKES to give them a buttermilk-esque flavor (buttermilk has become hard to find in shops, especially in London). The Seed Mix adds flavor, texture, and nutrients! My kids adore these and ask for them lots, especially my boy.

1 organic large egg

1¼ cups soy milk

¼ cup plus 1 tablespoon vegetable oil

1 cup flour, your preference, any kind will work

1 teaspoon baking powder

3 tablespoons Seed Mix (page 222) (optional)

3 tablespoons plain yogurt

Real Vermont maple syrup, for serving

Whisk the egg, soy milk, and ¼ cup of vegetable oil together in a bowl. Stir in the flour, the baking powder, and the Seed Mix until just combined (overbeating is how you get tough pancakes). Fold in the yogurt. Heat a large nonstick skillet or griddle over medium-high heat with the 1 tablespoon of vegetable oil (or you could use butter…or if you use Jamie Oliver's unbelievable slippery nonstick cookware you don't need any fat). Ladle as many pancakes as possible onto your skillet. Cook for about 2 minutes on the first side, or until the surface is covered with small bubbles and the underside is nicely browned. Flip and cook for about a minute on the second side. Remove the pancakes to a plate. Repeat the process until you run out of batter. Serve the pancakes stacked high with plenty of maple syrup.

 YIELD: about 2 dozen 3-inch pancakes • ACTIVE & TOTAL PREPARATION TIME: 15–20 minutes

seed mix

THIS IS A FANTASTIC WAY to give yourself and your kids essential nutrients. Top oatmeal, granola, applesauce (or anything!) for a crunchy texture and delicious flavor. You can also stir this mix into pancake, muffin, or cookie batters. Keep it in a jar in the refrigerator—it lasts for weeks.

1 part each pumpkin and sunflower seeds

2 parts each almonds, goji berries, and flaxseeds

Finely grind everything together in a mini food processor or coffee grinder in batches if necessary.

 YIELD: flexible · ACTIVE & TOTAL PREPARATION TIME: 5 minutes

homemade turkey sausage patties

I FIRST FEATURED THIS on my online newsletter GOOP for a holiday brunch menu. I wanted to create a healthy, organic sausage pattie that was not full of mystery meat, preservatives, and the like. These have become a real breakfast favorite at our house, so I had to include them here.

1 teaspoon fennel seeds

Pinch hot chile flakes

Pinch cayenne pepper

Pinch herbes de Provence salt (optional)

½ teaspoon coarse salt

¼ teaspoon freshly ground black pepper

1 teaspoon finely chopped fresh sage

½ pound ground turkey

2 teaspoons real Vermont maple syrup

2 tablespoons extra virgin olive oil

Using a mortar and pestle, a Flavour Shaker (gotta love Jamie Oliver), or mini food processor, bash the fennel seeds, chile flakes, cayenne, salts, and pepper together. Combine this spice mixture with the sage, turkey, and maple syrup in a bowl until thoroughly combined.

Form the mixture into small, thin patties. Heat the olive oil in a large nonstick pan over medium-high heat. Cook the sausages for about 1½ minutes on each side, pressing down with your spatula to really brown them and keep them thin. Serve warm.

make it kid friendly You can make these without the chile and cayenne for the kids.

YIELD: 1 dozen small patties • ACTIVE & TOTAL PREPARATION TIME: 15 minutes

You can even freeze the cooked patties and reheat them in the oven.

spiced apple crumb muffins

THESE NEXT TWO MUFFIN RECIPES are based on my friend Darlene's healthy recipes. D, as I call her, is a master at baking with alternative ingredients. The spelt flour has more nutritional value than regular wheat flour and it is easier to digest to boot. These are macrobiotic and super healthy, and my kids, as well as all visitors, gobble them up.

for the crumb topping

- ¼ cup white spelt flour
- ¼ cup whole spelt flour
- ¼ cup whole rolled oats (not instant and not steel-cut)
- ¼ cup unrefined dark brown sugar
- 2 teaspoons ground cinnamon
-   Pinch sea salt
- 2 tablespoons vegetable oil
- 1 tablespoon soy milk

for the muffins

- 1 tablespoon cornstarch
- 1 cup finely diced peeled apple (about 2 small apples)
- ½ cup vegetable oil, plus 2 tablespoons for greasing pan
- ½ cup plus 2 tablespoons real Vermont maple syrup
- ½ cup plus 2 tablespoons soy milk
- 1 cup white spelt flour
- 1 cup whole spelt flour
- 2¼ teaspoons baking powder
- ½ teaspoon baking soda
- ¼ teaspoon fine salt
- 2 teaspoons ground cinnamon
- ½ teaspoon ground allspice
- ½ cup lightly toasted walnuts, roughly chopped

Preheat the oven to 350°F. Line a 12-cup muffin tin with papers or oil it with two tablespoons of the vegetable oil.

For the crumb topping, combine all the dry ingredients in a small bowl. Add the vegetable oil and soy milk and rub everything together with your fingers—the mixture should be pebbly. Set the mixture aside.

For the muffins, in a small bowl, toss the cornstarch with the apples. In another large bowl, whisk together ½ cup of the vegetable oil and all of the syrup and soy milk. Sift in the remaining ingredients (except for the walnuts) and fold in the apples and walnuts. Evenly distribute the batter in the muffin cups and bake for 25–30 minutes, or until a toothpick tests clean.

YIELD: 1 dozen muffins · ACTIVE PREPARATION TIME: 15 minutes
TOTAL PREPARATION TIME: 45 minutes

banana walnut muffins

¼ cup plus 2 tablespoons
  canola oil

1 cup whole spelt flour

1 cup white spelt flour

½ cup barley flour

1 teaspoon baking soda

1 teaspoon fine salt

3 very ripe medium bananas

½ cup real Vermont maple
  syrup

¼ cup brown rice syrup

1 tablespoon vanilla extract

½ cup raisins

½ cup toasted walnuts,
  chopped

Preheat the oven to 350°F. Line a 12-cup muffin tin with papers or oil them with 2 tablespoons of the canola oil.

Sift the flours, baking soda, and salt into a medium-sized bowl. Puree the bananas in a food processor or blender and then add the ¼ cup of canola oil, syrups, and vanilla and pulse to combine. Make a well in the flour mixture and pour in the liquid mixture. Stir just to combine and fold in the raisins and walnuts (don't overmix or you will have tough muffins!). Use an ice cream scoop to distribute the batter evenly among the muffin cups. Bake for approximately 25 minutes, or until a toothpick tests clean. Cool in the pan for a few minutes before removing to a cooling rack.

YIELD: 1 dozen muffins • ACTIVE PREPARATION TIME: 15 minutes
TOTAL PREPARATION TIME: 45 minutes

favorite granola

I LOVE CLASSIC GRANOLA as much as the next person and this version is pepped up with some Indian spice. It's got a bit of a kick to it.

2 cups whole rolled oats (not instant and not steel-cut)

½ cup raw, whole almonds

¼ cup pumpkin seeds

¼ cup sunflower seeds

½ teaspoon garam masala

¼ teaspoon ground cinnamon

¼ teaspoon fine salt

½ cup real Vermont maple syrup

3 tablespoons light agave nectar or brown rice syrup

2 tablespoons vegetable oil

½ cup dried cranberries, roughly chopped

Preheat the oven to 350°F.

Stir together the oats, almonds, pumpkin and sunflower seeds, spices, and salt in a large bowl. Combine the maple syrup, agave, and vegetable oil in a small bowl and then mix with the dry ingredients. Spread the granola out on a nonstick sheet pan or a regular sheet pan covered with parchment paper and coated with a little vegetable oil. Bake for 15–20 minutes, stirring occasionally, or until evenly browned. If you like your granola in clumps, remove the pan from the oven and push the granola so it's about ⅓-inch thick, letting it cool completely and then breaking it apart into small pieces. If you like your granola loose, simply spread it out in the pan and let it cool. Either way, combine the cooled granola with the cranberries. It keeps well for 2–3 months in an airtight container.

YIELD: about 3 cups · ACTIVE PREPARATION TIME: 10 minutes
TOTAL PREPARATION TIME: ½ hour plus cooling

blythe's blueberry muffins

THE BEST EVER. I GREW UP eating my mother's perfect blueberry muffins—they set an unbeatable standard—just the right balance of tart and sweet. When I was pregnant with my daughter, I asked my mother to make them for me all the time.

8 tablespoons (1 stick) unsalted butter, melted and cooled

2 organic large eggs

½ cup milk

2 cups unbleached all-purpose flour

¾ cup plus 1 teaspoon granulated sugar

2 teaspoons baking powder

½ teaspoon fine salt

2½ cups fresh blueberries

Preheat the oven to 375°F. Line a 12-cup muffin tin with papers.

Whisk the butter, eggs, and milk together in a bowl. In another bowl, whisk together the flour, the ¾ cup of sugar, baking powder, and salt. Stir the wet ingredients into the dry ingredients and fold in the blueberries. Divide among the muffin cups and sprinkle the muffins with the remaining teaspoon of sugar. Bake until a toothpick tests clean and the muffins are golden brown, 25–30 minutes. Best to eat these warm.

YIELD: 1 dozen muffins · ACTIVE PREPARATION TIME: 15 minutes
TOTAL PREPARATION TIME: 45 minutes

healthier version of the
blueberry muffins

THESE MUFFINS MADE FROM SPELT flour don't have any sugar and are
vegan. They still rock the house.

½ cup vegetable oil

½ cup soy milk

½ cup real Vermont maple
    syrup

¼ cup light agave nectar

1 cup white spelt flour

1 cup whole spelt flour

2 teaspoons baking powder

½ teaspoon fine salt

2½ cups fresh blueberries

Preheat the oven to 375°F. Line a 12-cup muffin tin with papers.
    Mix wet ingredients together, stir in the dry ingredients, and fold in the blueberries. Divide among the muffin cups and bake until a toothpick tests clean and the muffins are golden brown, 25–30 minutes. Let cool before eating (if you can…).

YIELD: 1 dozen muffins · ACTIVE PREPARATION TIME: 15 minutes
TOTAL PREPARATION TIME: 45 minutes

challah french toast

MY BREAKFAST SPECIALTY. My family has asked me to make this at all hours of the day. The challah bread is the perfect texture and flavor for French toast—it's unbeatable in my opinion.

1 vanilla pod or 1 teaspoon vanilla extract (use the pod to make Vanilla Bean Sugar, page 31)

2 organic large eggs

1 cup milk

8 ¾-inch-thick slices challah bread or brioche

2 tablespoons unsalted butter

1 teaspoon coarse sugar

1 banana, peeled

Powdered sugar, for serving

Real Vermont maple syrup, for serving

Slice the vanilla pod in half lengthwise. Use the tip of a paring knife to scrape out all of the beans. Place the beans in a bowl with a teaspoon of hot water, and mix. Then crack the eggs into the bowl and whisk to blend, breaking up the sticky vanilla beans. Whisk the milk in. Dip the bread into the egg mixture, coating each slice on both sides.

Meanwhile, melt the butter in a large skillet over medium-high heat and add as many pieces of challah as can fit comfortably. Sprinkle the top of each piece with a tiny bit of coarse sugar. Cook for about 2 minutes, or until the underside is golden brown and the coating is crisp and lacy. Flip and sprinkle the cooked sides with a tiny bit of coarse sugar. Cook for about a minute or 2 longer, or until the second side is browned. Remove the French toast to a platter and repeat the process until all the pieces are cooked. Thinly slice the banana over the French toast, dust everything with powdered sugar, and serve with lots and lots of maple syrup.

SERVES: 4 • ACTIVE & TOTAL PREPARATION TIME: 15 minutes

savory rice bowl

NOW WE'RE TALKING. I LOVE a savory breakfast—and this is right up my alley. I first had a version of this at a Japanese monastery during a silent retreat—don't ask, it's a long story. Anyway it was a great (interesting) experience but the savory rice bowl was the best part. I came home and re-created it.

1 cup short-grain brown rice

6 cups water, divided

Soy sauce, for serving

Toasted sesame oil, for serving

Sesame and seaweed rice condiment (available at any Japanese grocery), for serving

Finely chopped scallions, for serving

Finely chopped kimchi, for serving

Finely shredded nori, for serving

Rinse off the rice and combine with 5 cups of the water in a saucepan. Bring to a boil, turn the heat as low as it can go, cover, and cook for 1½ hours. The rice should be very soft. Add the remaining 1 cup of water and cook for an additional 15–30 minutes. The mixture should be porridgelike.

To serve, spoon the rice into four bowls and top with the remaining ingredients, to suit your taste.

SERVES: 4 · ACTIVE PREPARATION TIME: 5 minutes · TOTAL PREPARATION TIME: 2 hours

OPPOSITE: Savory Rice Bowl (top),
Sweet Rice Bowl (bottom)

sweet rice bowl

I LOVE THIS WARM, dreamy maple syrup–drenched rice porridge. Sometimes when I'm pressed for time I just heat up some leftover brown rice from the fridge with a bit of rice milk and top it the same way. A wonderful wholesome way to start the day.

1 cup short-grain brown rice

6 cups water, divided

Real Vermont maple syrup, for serving

⅓ cup almonds for serving (I like them whole and raw, but roasted and chopped is pretty great too.)

Rinse off the rice and combine with 5 cups of the water in a saucepan. Bring to a boil, turn the heat as low as it can go, cover, and cook for 1½ hours. The rice should be very soft. Add the remaining 1 cup of water and cook for an additional 15–30 minutes. The mixture should be porridgelike.

To serve, spoon the rice into four bowls and top with the almonds and as much maple syrup as you like.

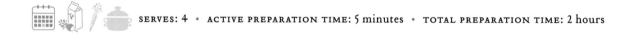 SERVES: 4 • ACTIVE PREPARATION TIME: 5 minutes • TOTAL PREPARATION TIME: 2 hours

oatmeal

A PIPING HOT BOWL of oats can be so right in the morning, especially topped with pure Vermont maple syrup, some berries, or my healthy seed mix—or whatever toppings you love. Instead of making it with whole milk, I use soy milk, almond milk, rice milk, or water (depending on the customer).

1 cup whole rolled oats (not instant and not steel-cut)

3 cups water, soy, almond, rice, or regular milk

Small pinch salt

Blueberries, blackberries, sliced bananas, almonds, raisins, maple syrup, flaxseeds, and/or Seed Mix (page 222)—whatever toppings you love

Combine the oats, water, and salt in a saucepan and set over medium heat. Bring to a simmer and cook, stirring, for 5-7 minutes, or until desired consistency is achieved. Serve with your favorite topping or combination of toppings.

SERVES: 4 • **ACTIVE & TOTAL PREPARATION TIME:** 10 minutes

This is vegan if soy, almond, or rice milk is used in place of regular milk.

bruce paltrow's world-famous pancakes

NOW IF THERE IS ONE IMAGE of my father that is the most "him"—that is to say encapsulates all of his elements and delivers them in one picture—it would be him over his cast-iron griddles making his world-famous pancakes. These things have been legendary in our house for decades. He first got the recipe out of the *Joy of Cooking* and adapted it over the years to utter perfection. The recipe below is so truthful to his pancakes that it's almost hard for me to eat them, I keep expecting him to walk into the kitchen.

3 cups unbleached all-purpose flour

¼ cup plus 2 tablespoons granulated sugar

1 tablespoon plus ½ teaspoon baking powder

2 teaspoons fine salt

3 cups buttermilk

6 tablespoons unsalted butter, melted and cooled, plus more butter for cooking

6 organic large eggs

Up to 1 cup milk, as needed to thin batter

Real Vermont maple syrup, warmed, for serving

Whisk the dry ingredients together in a large bowl. Whisk the buttermilk, butter, and eggs together in another bowl. Add the wet ingredients to the dry ingredients, whisking just enough to combine (small lumps are okay). Let the batter sit, covered, overnight. The next morning, heat up your griddle or favorite nonstick pan and slick it with a little butter. Add enough milk to the batter to thin it to the right consistency—the thicker the batter, the thicker and heavier your pancakes; the thinner the batter, the more delicate your pancakes—neither is wrong. Cook the pancakes on the griddle, flipping them after bubbles appear on the surface of the uncooked side. Let cook 2-3 minutes more, then remove, and eat with lots of warm maple syrup.

 YIELD: 3 dozen 5-inch pancakes • ACTIVE PREPARATION TIME: 20 minutes
TOTAL PREPARATION TIME: 20 minutes plus overnight resting

blythe's savory bread pudding

MY MOM USED TO MAKE THIS when company would come for an elegant, relaxed brunch. As this could be prepared before the doorbell rang, she could set everything up and enjoy herself once the guests arrived. It's very rich, so it's not great for an everyday breakfast. It's best to cut the richness with a mimosa....

4 cups ½-inch bread cubes (I use a foot-long loaf of soft French bread with the crusts removed.)

2 tablespoons extra virgin olive oil

Coarse salt

4 organic large eggs

¾ cup heavy cream

2 teaspoons fresh thyme leaves, minced

¼ teaspoon freshly ground black pepper

A little butter for the pan

½ cup grated sharp Cheddar cheese

Preheat the oven to 375°F.

Spread the bread cubes out on a cookie sheet, drizzle evenly with the olive oil, and sprinkle with a large pinch of salt. Bake for 7–8 minutes, stirring halfway through, or until lightly browned and crispy.

While the bread cubes are cooling, whisk together the eggs, cream, thyme, pepper, and a pinch of salt. Stir the bread cubes into the custard mixture and let it sit for at least 10 minutes (up to overnight).

Turn the oven down to 350°F.

Pour the mixture into a buttered 9-inch cake pan or 8-inch square pan (or divide it evenly among individual ramekins). Sprinkle the cheese on top and bake for 20 minutes, or until the cheese is bubbling and lightly browned. Serve warm.

SERVES: 4–6 · ACTIVE PREPARATION TIME: 25 minutes
TOTAL PREPARATION TIME: at least 45 minutes

This can be made ahead up until the point of baking.

scrambled eggs with smoked salmon & cream cheese

THIS IS A GREAT BREAKFAST dish when you are feeding a group. You can always leave out the salmon for the kids, but they love the cream cheese and chives.

8   organic large eggs
    Splash milk
    Big pinch coarse salt
    A few fresh grinds black pepper
    Big knob unsalted butter
⅓   pound smoked salmon, torn into bite-sized pieces
⅓   cup cream cheese
2   teaspoons finely sliced fresh chives, for serving

Whisk the eggs together with the milk, salt, and pepper. Melt the butter in a large nonstick skillet over medium heat. Add the eggs, let them sit for 1 minute, turn the heat to medium-low, and push them gently with a wooden spoon for 1½ minutes, or until very soft curds form. Fold in the salmon, dot with the cream cheese, turn the heat as low as it can go, and cover the skillet for 1½ minutes, or until the cheese begins to get oozy. Sprinkle with chives and serve.

SERVES: 4 • ACTIVE & TOTAL PREPARATION TIME: 10 minutes

omelet

A FLUFFY, DINER-STYLE OMELET that can be dressed up however you like to please any member of the family.

1 tablespoon unsalted butter

3 organic large eggs, very well beaten

Coarse salt

Freshly ground black pepper

Whatever filling you like (grated cheese, cooked mushrooms, Slow-Roasted Tomatoes, page 32, etc.)

Heat the butter in a small nonstick skillet (6–7 inches in diameter) over medium heat. Add the eggs and season the top with a pinch of salt and a grind of pepper. Cover the skillet with a dinner plate and let them cook for 30 seconds. If you'd like to fill your omelet, at this point remove the plate and sprinkle over your desired filling, put the plate back on top, and cook for 30 more seconds. Take off the plate (incidentally, you now have a warm plate that will be perfect for the almost finished omelet) and tilt the skillet side to side to make sure the eggs are evenly cooked. Cook for about 30 seconds more and then slip a flexible spatula under half of the omelet and carefully fold it over the other half as if closing a book. Pat the omelet down, cook for 1 minute, and then flip the entire thing over with the spatula and cook for another 30–60 seconds. Remove the omelet from the skillet onto your warm plate, sprinkle with a tiny bit more salt and an extra grating of cheese if you'd like. This makes an omelet that's browned on the outside, but if you prefer something more gentle, simply turn the heat down a notch.

SERVES: 1 • **ACTIVE & TOTAL PREPARATION TIME:** 5 minutes

desserts

I came across an axiom in a passage from a culinary memoir called *Heat* in which the author, Bill Buford, observes the following: "You can divide people into two categories in life: cooks and bakers." I am definitely in the former category. In my mind, baking pastries, cookies, cakes, and the like is scientific—it allows for little improv. Some of my desserts require some baking but more of them are a bit more free-form and have room for adjustment to your personal taste. For me a dash of homemade hot fudge, a banana, and some roasted nuts over ice cream just hits the spot. More often than not when I prepare desserts, I am thinking about keeping the sugar intake low, as well as limiting other ingredients that don't do us any favors. I don't want to overload my kids with sugar seven days a week. With that in mind, many of these recipes, while tasting very decadent, are actually full of healthier ingredients. A cool trick that healthy baker Darlene Gross taught me.

fudgy chocolate brownies

THESE ARE ABOUT AS HEALTHY as brownies can get, with no flavor sacrifice.

2 cups white spelt flour

1 cup high-quality cocoa powder

1½ tablespoons baking powder

Pinch fine salt

½ cup vegetable oil

1 cup real Vermont maple syrup

½ cup brown rice syrup or light agave nectar

½ cup strong brewed coffee

½ cup soy milk

1 tablespoon vanilla extract

1 cup high-quality chocolate chips, divided (look for the grain-sweetened variety if you want to stay sugar free)

Preheat the oven to 350°F. Grease a baking dish (I use a 9 x 11-inch dish that's 2 inches high) with vegetable oil.

Sift the flour, cocoa, baking powder, and salt together in a large mixing bowl. In a separate bowl, whisk together the ½ cup of vegetable oil, syrups, coffee, soy milk, and vanilla. Mix the wet ingredients into the dry ingredients, being careful not to overbeat (that's how you end up with tough cake!). Pour half the batter into the baking dish. Sprinkle with half of the chocolate chips. Pour the rest of the batter into the baking dish, and sprinkle with the rest of the chocolate chips. Bake for 30 minutes (less if your pan is shallow, more if it's deep), or until a toothpick has just a bit of chocolate on it when you test the cake (this means it'll be super fudgy!). Let it cool if you have patience, cut into squares, and serve.

SERVES: about 8 • ACTIVE PREPARATION TIME: 15 minutes
TOTAL PREPARATION TIME: 45 minutes

grandad danner's favorite peanut butter cookies

BASED ON MY GRANDMOTHER'S very old recipe, these cookies are a slightly softer version of my granddad Danner's favorite peanut butter cookies. These were his favorite things on earth and my grandmother always made them for him. He passed away when I was seven, but I can still remember him with his thick shock of white hair eating these cookies with a glass of milk.

1¼ cups unbleached all-purpose flour

½ teaspoon baking soda

½ teaspoon baking powder

½ teaspoon fine salt

8 tablespoons (1 stick) unsalted butter, at room temperature

¾ cup smooth peanut butter, at room temperature

½ cup firmly packed dark brown sugar

½ cup firmly packed light brown sugar

1 organic large egg, at room temperature

1 teaspoon vanilla extract

1 cup peanut butter chips

¼ cup granulated sugar (optional)

Preheat oven to 350°F.

Whisk together the dry ingredients in a medium bowl. In a large bowl, cream together the butter, peanut butter, and brown sugars. Stir in the egg and vanilla. Add the flour in thirds and stir until smooth. Fold in the peanut butter chips. Roll the mixture into golf ball–sized balls (about 1½ tablespoons). At this point you can roll them in granulated sugar or you can press each cookie down with the tines of a fork. Either way, bake for 10 minutes, in a nonstick baking pan, rotating the pan halfway through baking time. Cool the cookies on a rack before serving.

YIELD: about 30 cookies · **ACTIVE PREPARATION TIME:** 10 minutes
TOTAL PREPARATION TIME: 20 minutes

oatmeal raisin cookies

THESE ARE MY ABSOLUTE FAVORITE healthy treat. They are so guilt free they can hardly be called cookies, except they taste delicious.

½ cup raisins

¾ cup toasted walnuts

1 cup whole rolled oats (not instant and not steel-cut), divided

½ cup white spelt flour

¾ cup whole spelt flour

1½ teaspoons ground cinnamon

1 teaspoon baking soda

½ teaspoon fine salt

⅓ cup vegetable oil

⅓ cup real Vermont maple syrup

⅓ cup brown rice syrup

2 teaspoons vanilla extract

Preheat the oven to 350°F. Line baking sheets with parchment paper.

Place the raisins in a small bowl and cover with boiling water to plump them.

Meanwhile, finely grind the walnuts and ½ cup of the oats in a small food processor. Combine this mixture with the remaining dry ingredients in a large mixing bowl. Mix together the wet ingredients in a small bowl and add to the dry-ingredients bowl. Stir to combine. Drain the raisins and fold them into the batter. Drop the mixture by large spoonfuls onto the baking sheets. Bake for 13–15 minutes until browned. Remove to a cooling rack.

YIELD: about 18 cookies · **ACTIVE PREPARATION TIME:** 15 minutes
TOTAL PREPARATION TIME: ½ hour

"I don't have a sweet tooth. *All* my teeth are sweet."
—MOSES

homemade root beer floats

WHEN I WAS GROWING UP, my dad used to take me to the A&W drive-in for hot dogs and his favorite sweet dessert refreshment on earth, the root beer float. My dad was a root beer man and drilled into me the fine attributes of the soda early in life. It's only when I grew up and read the side of the can that I became disillusioned about enjoying it regularly. I wondered how difficult it would be to make my own organic version, devoid of corn syrup. As it turned out, not difficult at all. The day we were finding the formula, my daughter, who was four years old at the time, walked into the kitchen and asked me what I was drinking. "Soda," I replied. She looked at me with her big blue eyes. "What's that?" she responded. With this version, I felt good about letting her discover it for herself.

2 cups water

2 cloves

8 peppercorns

¼ cup sassafras extract

¼ cup unrefined dark brown sugar

2-inch piece fresh ginger, peeled and crushed with the back of your knife

Carbonated water

4 scoops vanilla ice cream

Combine the water, cloves, peppercorns, sassafras, sugar, and ginger together in a small pot. Bring to a boil, lower the heat, and simmer until a nice syrup forms, about 10 minutes. Let the syrup cool, strain out the solids, and then divide it between four small glasses. Dilute it with carbonated water so the soda reaches your desired strength (I like about ⅔ cup). Drop a scoop of ice cream into each glass. Heaven.

note: You can order sassafras extract from Flower Power Herbs & Roots (a funky store in NYC's East Village, visit flowerpower.net).

SERVES: 4 • ACTIVE PREPARATION TIME: 10 minutes
TOTAL PREPARATION TIME: 15 minutes plus cooling

lalo's famous cookies

LALO (AS MY MOTHER is affectionately called by my children—who wants to be called Grandma anyway?) is famous far and wide for these delicious cookies. They are incredibly good for you—I even let my kids have them with breakfast—not a bad ingredient in the bunch. I use a nonstick pan for baking.

4   cups barley flour

3   cups raw whole almonds crushed in a food processor (about ten 2-second pulses)

1   teaspoon fine salt

1   teaspoon ground cinnamon

1   cup canola oil

1   cup real Vermont maple syrup

Your favorite jam (blueberry, raspberry, and apricot are all very nice)

Preheat the oven to 350°F.

Combine all the ingredients except for the jam together in a large bowl with a wooden spoon. Form into tablespoonful balls and space them evenly on cookie sheets. Using your index finger, make an indent in each cookie. Fill each indent with a small spoonful of jam. Bake until cookies are evenly browned, about 20 minutes. Let cool before eating.

YIELD: about 50 cookies · ACTIVE PREPARATION TIME: 25 minutes
TOTAL PREPARATION TIME: 45 minutes

pomegranate granita

GRANITA IS AN EASY WAY to have a lovely, healthy, refreshing dessert. I like this one—Granita Granada as I like to call it (*granada* means "pomegranate" in Spanish). No sugar, no dairy, all goodness.

2 cups fresh pomegranate juice

1 tablespoon fresh lemon juice

¼ cup light agave nectar

¼ cup fresh pomegranate seeds

Whisk together the juices and agave and pour into an 8-inch metallic pie pan or another similar-sized vessel. Freeze for 1 hour. Take out of the freezer and scrape with a fork. Repeat this process every 15 minutes for the next 2 hours. You should end up with a solid mixture that resembles flakes of sorbet. Alternatively, you can freeze it overnight and scrape it before serving. To serve, scoop into six glasses or bowls and sprinkle with the fresh pomegranate seeds.

note: To get the most flavor and brilliant color, only use 100 percent pomegranate juice from the refrigerated section of the grocery store.

SERVES: 6 · ACTIVE PREPARATION TIME: 15 minutes · TOTAL PREPARATION TIME: 3 hours

margarita granita

NOT A GRANITA FOR THE KIDDIES—this is a fun dessert for a grown-up dinner party or as an aperitif in a little cup on a summer night.

Zest of 1 lime
½ cup fresh lime juice
(4–5 medium limes)
¼ cup light agave nectar
1 cup water
¼ cup highest-quality tequila

Whisk everything together and pour into an 8-inch metallic pie pan or another similar-sized vessel. Freeze for 1 hour. Take out of the freezer and scrape with a fork. Repeat this process every 15 minutes for the next 2 hours. You should end up with a solid mixture that resembles flakes of sorbet. Alternatively, you can freeze it overnight and scrape it before serving. To serve, scoop into six glasses (salt the rims if you'd like).

SERVES: 6 • ACTIVE PREPARATION TIME: 15 minutes • TOTAL PREPARATION TIME: 3 hours

mutti's pecan butterballs

MY GRANDMOTHER MUTTI WAS—how shall I say this?—a unique person. She shone when she was entertaining—cooking, singing, baking. These butterballs were the big treat in our house at Christmastime. Mutti would lovingly make and roll the balls and they would disappear. Careful not to inhale the powdered sugar!

16 tablespoons (2 sticks) unsalted butter, at room temperature

2 cups pecans, finely chopped or pulsed in a food processor

2½ cups unbleached all-purpose flour

Pinch fine salt

½ cup plus 2 tablespoons powdered sugar

Preheat oven to 350°F.

Mix everything, except the ½ cup of sugar together in a mixing bowl with your hands. Roll tablespoonfuls into balls and place on 2 nonstick cookie sheets. Bake for 20 minutes, rotating the sheets halfway through baking. When they're nearly cool, gently roll each ball in the ½ cup of sugar. Put the leftover sugar in a sieve and shake over the cookies. These keep well in a tin, for a week.

YIELD: about 50 cookies · ACTIVE PREPARATION TIME: 25 minutes
TOTAL PREPARATION TIME: 45 minutes

blueberry pavlova

PAVLOVA IS EASY AND KIND of foolproof. Just use fresh ripe blueberries, or any kind you like really—it's so delicious with meringue. I like to make this after I make homemade pasta so I don't waste the egg whites.

4   organic large egg whites
    Pinch fine salt
½   teaspoon white vinegar
¾   cup plus 2 tablespoons granulated sugar
1   tablespoon cornstarch
½   teaspoon vanilla extract
1   cup heavy cream
1½ cups fresh blueberries, plus more for serving

Preheat the oven to 350°F.

Combine egg whites, salt, and white vinegar together in the bowl of an electric mixer and beat on high speed until soft peaks form. Combine the ¾ cup sugar and cornstarch together in a small bowl and add to the egg whites in thirds, whisking each addition in completely. Add the vanilla and beat until stiff peaks form.

Line a baking sheet with parchment paper and spoon the meringue in 8 big spoonfuls, using a spoon to spread them in a circle, and then make an indent in each. Bake for 10 minutes, lower the heat to 200°F, and bake for another hour. Turn off the heat and cool the meringues in the oven for an hour, propping the door open with a wooden spoon.

Meanwhile, whip the cream together with the remaining 2 tablespoons of sugar. In a small bowl, crush ½ cup of the blueberries with a potato masher or a spoon to release their juice. Fold those and the rest of the blueberries into the cream if you like, or use as a topping over the egg whites and cream. Evenly distribute the cream on the meringues, filling in the indentations. Top with juicy blueberries and serve.

 SERVES: 8 • **ACTIVE PREPARATION TIME:** 15 minutes • **TOTAL PREPARATION TIME:** 2½ hours

berries with caramelized cream

ONE EVENING WHEN I HAD my wood-burning stove going
I realized I hadn't thought of dessert. I found some frozen berries in the
freezer and since I didn't have time to make a cobbler, I whipped up a sweet
cream topping for the berries and whacked them in the oven. The cream
topping went all lovely and brown and the whole thing was made and done in
about seven minutes.

2 pints blueberries, blackberries, and/or raspberries

2 tablespoons sour cream

2 tablespoons heavy cream

1 organic large egg

1 organic egg white

1 cup mascarpone

3 tablespoons powdered sugar

Pinch fine sea salt

Seeds of 1 vanilla bean (use the scraped bean for your Vanilla Bean Sugar, page 31)

Preheat the broiler and put the oven rack in the middle or lower half of your oven.

Put the berries in a pie or casserole dish. Whisk together the remaining ingredients until completely smooth and pour over the berries. Put the dish in the oven and cook just until the topping is browned and caramelized, 5–10 minutes.

SERVES: 6 · ACTIVE & TOTAL PREPARATION TIME: 10 minutes

This can be made ahead up until the point of broiling.

seasonal crumble

ONE OF MY ABSOLUTE FAVORITE things to do with my children is to pick fruit for crumble, a dessert we love. We never seem to have enough of any one berry all at the same time, so we either do mixed berries or peaches in the summer, and apple in the autumn. This is a fantastic thing to do if you can pick fruit somewhere and have your kids participate in the whole process. From washing the fruit to mixing and assembling, they can actually make the whole thing virtually by themselves. They will really get a sense of where everything comes from and the steps we take to turn it into something delicious. This recipe utilizes the sweetness of the fruit, cutting down on added sugar, always a good thing.

4	cups fruit (sliced peaches, diced apples, blackberries, blueberries, etc.)
¼	cup plus 1 tablespoon white spelt flour
1	cup whole rolled oats (not instant and not steel-cut)
¼	cup firmly packed unrefined dark brown sugar
¼	teaspoon ground cinnamon
	Pinch fine salt
4	tablespoons unsalted butter, at room temperature
	Ice cream, for serving

Preheat the oven to 350°F.

Combine the fruit with the 1 tablespoon of flour in a 9-inch pie pan or similar-sized baking dish. Combine the rest of the ingredients (except the ice cream) together in a mixing bowl, using your hands to form pea-sized crumbs. Sprinkle the topping evenly over the fruit. Bake for 45 minutes, or until the topping is browned and the fruit juices are bubbling. Serve warm with ice cream.

 SERVES: 6 · ACTIVE PREPARATION TIME: 15 minutes · TOTAL PREPARATION TIME: 1 hour

This can be made ahead up until the point of baking.

my favorite homemade hot fudge

BROWN RICE SYRUP, THOUGH LESS COMMON than corn syrup, is worth seeking out because it lends the fudge a rounder, smoother, less saccharine flavor and it's also a lot better for you. If you can't find it, light corn syrup is totally okay to use and I've even found organic varieties. This is perfect over ice cream or as a dip for fruit, especially good with strawberries and bananas.

3 ounces semisweet dark chocolate (62 percent), finely chopped

¼ cup heavy cream

2 tablespoons brown rice syrup (or light corn syrup)

Combine all of the ingredients in a double boiler (or in a metal or glass bowl set above a small pot of simmering water) and stir until completely melted, about 3 minutes. Serve warm.

SERVES: 4 · **ACTIVE & TOTAL PREPARATION TIME:** 5 minutes

RELIABLE ONLINE RESOURCES

adrianascaravan.com for chiles and spices

asianfoodgrocer.com for Asian ingredients

bobsredmill.com for flours and grains, especially
great for alternative flours such as gluten-free
baking mix, barley flour, and buckwheat flour

dartagnan.com for duck bacon and confit

flowerpower.net for sassafras extract

kalustyans.com for spices, grains, and sauces,
especially anything Indian

penzeys.com for spices and chiles

tienda.com for Spanish ingredients and tools

acknowledgments

I am indebted to the lovely and inspirational Ellen Silverman for her beautiful photos, Susie Theodorou for the food styling and good humor, Sara Slavin for the prop styling, and everyone else who helped make the photo production a reality: Nick Duers, Rebecca Jurkevich, Kristin Knauff, Amy Neunsinger and family, Loren Simpson, Leslie Lopez, Adir Abergel, Ashlie Johnson, and Meyler & Company. And for the cover shoot: Lucy Attwater, Renato Campora, Kristofer Buckle, Kevin Norris, and, of course, Ellen.

Additional gratitude to Harold Brown, Luke Janklow, Dani Wells-Cole, and the truly amazing Cleo Brock-Abraham. And to Stephen Huvane for twenty years of support.

Karen Murgolo and the team at Grand Central Publishing, including Matthew Ballast, Philippa White, Tareth Mitch, Anne Twomey, and Claire Brown. And to Laura Palese, for a beautiful design.

And of course…Georgie, Eliza, Kevin, Elouisa, Reina, Ljube, Victoria and Julio, Aimee, Marta, Laura, Leticia, and the wonderful Terry Abbot.

And a special thank you to Rochelle Udell, who came up with the title for this book.

I tip my hat to the chefs, home cooks, food authors, and restaurateurs who have been my teachers…starting with my dear friend and professor of all things, Mario Batali. The chef friends of my parents who opened up the culinary world to us Paltrows—the late Sheila Lukins, one of my mother's closest friends, for her wonderful eccentricity in the kitchen and out; Michael and Kim McCarty, our conduit to the food revolution in California; Jonathan Waxman; and Gordon Naccarato. Lee and Darlene Gross, who taught me more than anyone about healthy eating; Jamie Oliver, for one of the best cooking lessons imaginable. Arjun Waney for his incredible kitchens and friendship. The Elio's kitchen, the Chez L'Ami Louis kitchen, and of course the inimitable Ruthie Rogers and the River Cafe kitchen.

credits Sue Fisher King (San Francisco), D'Artagnan, TableArt (Los Angeles), Unici (West Hollywood), Rina Menardi (Los Angeles)

index

about the author

Gwyneth Paltrow is an Oscar-winning actress, founder of GOOP.com, co-author with Mario Batali of *Spain, A Culinary Road Trip,* and mother of two. She splits her time between London and New York.